The Evolution Debate
Darwinism vs. Intelligent Design

ISSUES IN FOCUS TODAY

Sherri Mabry Gordon

Enslow Publishers, Inc.
40 Industrial Road
Box 398
Berkeley Heights, NJ 07922
USA
http://www.enslow.com

Library of Congress Cataloging-in-Publication Data

Gordon, Sherri Mabry.
    The evolution debate : Darwinism vs. intelligent design / Sherri Mabry Gordon.
        p. cm. — (Issues in focus today)
    Summary: "Discusses the debate between teaching evolution and intelligent design in
schools, including the history of teaching Darwinism in science classes, and the arguments from both sides of the issue"—Provided by publisher.
    Includes bibliographical references and index.
    ISBN-13: 978-0-7660-2911-8
    ISBN-10: 0-7660-2911-5
    1. Evolution (Biology)—Juvenile literature. 2. Intelligent design (Teleology)—
Juvenile literature. I. Title.
QH367.1.G67 2009
576.8—dc22

                                    2008017416

Printed in the United States of America

10 9 8 7 6 5 4 3 2 1

To Our Readers: We have done our best to make sure all Internet addresses in this book were
active and appropriate when we went to press. However, the author and the publisher have
no control over and assume no liability for the material available on those Internet sites or on
other Web sites they may link to. Any comments or suggestions can be sent by e-mail to com-
ments@enslow.com or to the address on the back cover.

♲ Enslow Publishers, Inc., is committed to printing our books on recycled paper. The paper in
every book contains 10% to 30% post-consumer waste (PCW). The cover board on the outside
of each book contains 100% PCW. Our goal is to do our part to help young people and the
environment too!

Illustration Credits: Courtesy of Michael Behe, p. 39; EyeWire Images, p. 74; iStockphoto.com,
pp. 3, 20, 24, 105; Library of Congress, pp. 9, 12; courtesy of Kenneth Miller, p. 49;
Photos.com, pp. 3, 28, 58, 66, 78, 85, 90, 94, 113, 115, 117; Shutterstock, pp. 1, 3, 5, 33, 41,
45, 54, 81, 101, 109, 111; Wikimedia Commons, pp. 16, 98, 107.

Cover Illustration: Photos.com (teen boy with book); iStockphoto.com (statue of Charles
Darwin); BananaStock (very small inset photo).

C o n t e n t s

← **EVOLUTION**

INTELLIGENT DESIGN →

The Rivals: An Overview of the Controversy

Thirty-five years ago, when Samuel Jefferson was in high school in central Ohio, evolution was taught exclusively. Other ideas or theories about how different species originated were not mentioned. Creation, the belief that God created everything on Earth, was no longer being taught alongside evolution in his high school.

"You know, back when I was growing up things were always compartmentalized," he says. "You had your public school education, which was in my mind based on hard facts. And then on Sundays we went to Sunday school. That is where we heard the creation story. I never felt pressure from either side. I think I have background in both and then I made my own decisions from that point."

Jefferson, who is a newspaper editor and local historian, says he was taught the basics of evolution theory in high school. He also says it was not taught as an absolute.

"They always took great pains to show testing and give you examples, all the while saying it is still something that is ongoing," he says. "It is like the theory of evolution is evolving. It is constantly in a state of flux. As new things are found, it changes past thoughts and creates new ones."

Today, Jefferson says that he believes in God, but he leans more toward evolution as the method for the way different species originated.[1]

Twenty-five years later, when Erica and Josh Van Dop were in high school in central Ohio, their experiences were vastly different from Jefferson's. In fact, both the Van Dops had biology classes in which several ideas were discussed in addition to evolution. Even then their experiences were different.

For example, at Erica's high school the students brought ideas about creation into the evolution discussion. But the teacher did not encourage these discussions to continue and would not share her personal beliefs.

"We would openly try to introduce creationism there—even along the lines of the supernatural—and the conversations just got shut down," Erica says. "She only taught evolution and the big bang theory."

Erica, who now has an undergraduate degree in premed and a master's degree in health promotion, says the class's discussions were pretty lively, and finally the teacher allowed the students to organize a debate over evolution and creation.

"The teacher did not participate because she could not state her opinion," she says. "That was fine because we got to debate and say what we had to say and what we actually thought."

Josh, who has an undergraduate degree in biology, had a

completely different experience at his high school. His biology teacher presented both sides of the issue—evolution and intelligent design.

"[The teacher] was pretty well known in the school for his evolution teaching. This was the big topic of the school year," Josh says. "He just presented both sides in what I thought to be an unbiased setup within the classroom. We did that for several weeks and then at the end he told us what he thought and left it at that."

Josh says he really appreciated this approach because it allowed him to draw his own conclusions.

"[The teacher believed] in presenting both sides and letting people make their own decisions and not forcing [an opinion] on someone else," he explains. "I thought it really let all of us explore and work at what we thought the answer was and not just take what we thought our parents would think or what would be the 'right' answer for the class."

Today Erica and Josh, who both have science backgrounds and are Christians, accept some aspects of both theories. For example, Josh says he believes parts of evolution, especially that organisms change or adapt to their environment. But as far as how different species originated, he believes in creation. Erica shares a similar view.

"I feel like the two theories can run side by side," she says. "I do not agree with everything evolution states, but I think some of the principles could be incorporated. There is not a conflict with faith and evolution."[2]

The Battle Over Evolution Officially Begins

The controversy over evolution in this country began in the mid-1800s, when Charles Darwin suggested that humans were a product of evolution. However, it was not until the 1900s that the battle started to really heat up in America.

In July 1925, the world's attention was focused on Dayton,

Tennessee. At issue was the teaching of evolution in schools. Under the state's Butler Act, teaching evolution in the classroom was not allowed.

Until the late nineteenth century, creation was taught in nearly all schools in the United States. But as science continued to advance and the theory of evolution gained acceptance by the scientific community, more and more schools began to teach it.

The controversy over evolution in this country began in the mid-1800s, when Darwin suggested that humans were a product of evolution. However, it was not until the 1900s that the battle started to really heat up in America.

The American Civil Liberties Union (ACLU), an organization founded in 1920 to protect individuals' constitutional rights, hoped to get Tennessee's Butler Act thrown out. But to do so, they needed a teacher willing to see it through. As a result, they ran an ad in the *Chattanooga Daily News* looking for a teacher who was willing to help by standing trial.[3]

A local Dayton businessman, thirty-year-old George W. Rappalyea, the manager of the bankrupt Cumberland Coal and Iron Company, saw the ad. Although Rappalyea attended a Methodist church, he believed in the theory of evolution and did not like the new law. Additionally, his coal company was declining and he wanted a way to promote local business.[4]

Rappalyea felt that a trial in Dayton would do just that. After all, this trial would not be just any trial—it would attract a lot of attention. So he approached a gathering of town leaders to help him find a legal guinea pig.[5]

At the center of the trial was a young man named John Scopes—a teacher and a football coach. He reluctantly agreed to be arrested for teaching evolution. Scopes taught math and general science and sometimes served as a substitute for biology. He agreed to discuss evolution in class knowing that when he did, he would be arrested.[6]

Reporters coined the phrase the *Scopes Monkey Trial* because Darwin's theory was popularly interpreted to say that people descended from monkeys. And the title stuck. Even though the trial was named after Scopes, he did not grab the public's attention as much as the prosecutor, William Jennings Bryan, and the defense attorney, Clarence Darrow.

John Scopes (on left) with his father. The younger Scopes allowed himself to be used as a test case for the legality of teaching the theory of evolution.

Bryan was a Christian and a three-time presidential candidate who represented Tennessee. Darrow was an agnostic (one who says they do not know whether God exists), a Darwin supporter, and a legendary defense attorney. Both men were considered to be among the best debaters of their time. In fact, Darrow had been trying for years to publicly debate Bryan about science and religion. The Scopes trial would be his chance to do that.

People flocked to Dayton not only because of the trial but also to see Bryan and Darrow square off. More than two hundred journalists arrived to cover the trial. And it was the first American trial ever to be broadcast on the radio.

Toward the end of the trial, Bryan and Darrow still had not debated. So Darrow decided to try something different. He decided to call Bryan to the stand as an expert on the Bible. Although many people discouraged Bryan from taking the stand, he still agreed to be an expert witness. The debate between the nation's greatest public speakers was about to happen.

Darrow was relentless while questioning Bryan about events in the Bible. He fired off questions as he paced back and forth. Both men became frustrated and angry. Finally, Darrow got an answer from Bryan that he liked: Bryan admitted that he did not believe in a literal interpretation of the creation story found in the Bible. He also added that those who believed in a literal account weren't necessarily wrong either.[7]

The trial ended with the debate, because Darrow decided not to give a closing argument. When the defense does not give a closing statement, the prosecutor cannot give one either. Bryan was disappointed because he had spent seven weeks preparing his closing arguments.[8]

The trial lasted only nine days, and at the conclusion of the trial, the jury spent only nine minutes before finding Scopes guilty. The judge fined Scopes one hundred dollars. A

Baltimore newspaper representative paid the fine and Scopes was set free. The "trial of the century" was over.[9]

After the trial, Scopes gave up teaching. Instead, he studied geology at the University of Chicago. He paid for his education with scholarship money from a fund set up for him by a group of journalists and scientists. Scopes later enjoyed a successful career with the oil industry.[10]

Yet the story did not die there in the sweltering heat of that Tennessee courtroom. The trial was over, but the battle over what should be taught in America's science classrooms was just warming up.

The Significance of the Trial

The Scopes trial raised questions about the law, science, religion, philosophy, and politics. Experts say these questions will be debated for a long time to come.

"As a case it is not as much a legal landmark as much as a social landmark. It was a clash between traditionalism and its values and modernism and its values," says Douglas Linder of the University of Missouri–Kansas City law school, who teaches a seminar on famous trials. "Darwinism and evolution challenge the notion that we are special as a species."[11]

According to Edward Larson, author of *Summer for the Gods*, a book about the trial, the Tennessee Supreme Court overturned the decision on a technicality. The judge had set the fine when it was the jury that should have imposed the fine. What's more, the Supreme Court did not overturn the Butler Act as the ACLU had hoped. But it did say that Tennessee prosecutors should not charge anyone under the law.[12]

Although evolution continued to be taught in some Tennessee schools, Larson said many schools stayed away from the topic of evolution because it was so controversial.[13] In fact, a 1982 *Nature* article showed that references to Darwin and evolution in science books fell significantly after the Scopes trial. Some books eliminated the topic altogether, while others simply deleted it from the index.[14]

What's more, the textbook that Scopes used, *A Civic Biology*, was renamed *New Civic Biology* in 1926, and all references to evolution were removed. Things did not actually move in favor of evolution until the Cold War era, when the United States saw the launch of *Sputnik*, the Soviet Union's artificial satellite. Many people felt this launch was a sign that the Soviet Union was superior in science to the United States.[15]

The courtroom at the trial of John Scopes. Clarence Darrow, the defense attorney, is at the center (in suspenders).

Inherit the Wind: Fact or Fiction?

Inherit the Wind, written by Jerome Lawrence and Robert E. Lee, was loosely based on the Scopes trial. It enjoyed much success as a play, in movie theaters, and on television. The movie version, made in 1960, did not claim to show the trial exactly as it happened. But many people believed that it was mostly true because it was based on a true story. As a result, people do not always have an accurate picture of the trial.

There were numerous changes made in the making of the movie. The following are just a few of the things that are different from the actual trial:

- *Inherit the Wind* has a scene with Scopes in jail being threatened by people from his community. In actuality, Scopes spent no time in jail and was treated very well by Dayton residents, even though he had only lived there for a year.

- *Inherit the Wind* shows Scopes with no legal representation up to the day before his trial. In real life, Scopes had the promise of a good defense by the ACLU. In fact, he enjoyed the best legal defense team ever assembled for a misdemeanor trial in the United States.

- Bryan was portrayed in *Inherit the Wind* as a political hack and blustering buffoon. In real life, even Scopes described Bryan as "the greatest man produced in the United States since Thomas Jefferson."[16]

- It is commonly assumed that Dayton's science textbook was largely based on creation. This is not true. The book contained a great deal on evolution and did not mention anything about God, the Bible, or Adam and Eve.

- *Inherit the Wind* shows Darrow and Scopes nervously awaiting the verdict. In real life, Darrow asked the jury to find his client guilty and declined to give a closing argument.

Consequently, efforts were quickly made to update the country's science programs. All areas of science were affected, including biology. Evolution began to take on a bigger role in both textbooks and in classrooms. But it did not take opponents of evolution long to rally.[17]

The Battle Over Evolution Today

At issue today is the question of what should be taught in science class. This debate centers on the struggle for freedom of speech and the struggle for freedom of religion. Other issues within the debate include:

- evolution versus intelligent design

- separation of church and state and the Establishment Clause

- academic freedom and student rights

For example, intelligent design (ID) supporters hope that one day their theory will share the spotlight in science class with evolution. At the very least, they hope students will be exposed to the controversies surrounding the theory of evolution. They want students to examine both theories—evolution and intelligent design—critically.

Meanwhile, evolutionists are intent on defending their status in science. By no means do they plan to share the spotlight with an idea they consider "pseudoscience." The term *pseudoscience* implies that something is not truly a science, but an imposter. What's more, they are often unwilling to even debate the issue with opponents because they feel the theory of evolution is so well supported by evidence.

Both sides of the debate have some well-known thinkers and scientists. On the side of evolution, the most notable supporters include:

- **Richard Dawkins**—Dawkins was born in Nairobi, Kenya, in 1941 and educated at Oxford University. He taught zoology both at the University of California and at Oxford. Dawkins also has written a number of books related to evolution, including *The Selfish Gene*, *The Blind Watchmaker*, and *The God Delusion*.

- **Kenneth Miller**—Miller did his undergraduate work at Brown University and earned a PhD in 1974 at the University of Colorado. He spent six years as an assistant professor at Harvard University before returning to Brown as professor of biology. Miller's research work has produced more than fifty scientific papers and reviews in leading journals, and he is the coauthor of three high school and college biology textbooks. He also is the author of *Finding Darwin's God*.

- **Robert Pennock**—Pennock received his PhD in the history and philosophy of science from the University of Pittsburgh. Currently, he is a philosopher and associate professor at Michigan State University. Pennock has written many books and articles criticizing intelligent design, including *Tower of Babel* and *Intelligent Design Creationism and Its Critics*.

- **Eugenie Scott**—Scott studied at the University of Missouri–Columbia where she earned a PhD in anthropology. She is a physical anthropologist and the executive director of the National Center for Science Education. Scott also authored the book *Evolution vs. Creationism: An Introduction*.

Notable supporters on the side of intelligent design include:

- **Michael Behe**—Behe received a BS degree in chemistry from Drexel University and a PhD from the University of Pennsylvania. He is professor of biochemistry at

Lehigh University. Behe has authored more than forty technical articles and he is the author of *Darwin's Black Box: The Biochemical Challenge to Evolution.*

- **William Dembski**—Dembski is a graduate of the University of Illinois at Chicago, where he earned a BA in psychology, an MS in statistics, a PhD in philosophy, and a PhD in mathematics. He also received a master of divinity degree from Princeton Theological Seminary. Dembski has done postdoctoral work in mathematics at MIT, in physics at the University of Chicago, and in computer science at Princeton University. Dembski is the author of seven books, including *The Design Inference: Eliminating Chance Through Small Probabilities*, and *No Free Lunch: Why Specified Complexity Cannot Be Purchased Without Intelligence.*

- **Phillip Johnson**—Johnson received a bachelor's degree in English literature from Harvard University and studied law at the University of Chicago. Johnson is a retired University of California at Berkeley American law professor and author. Johnson is often considered the father of the intelligent design movement. His most notable books include *Darwin on Trial* and *Defeating Darwinism by Opening Minds.*

William Dembski, a prime defender of the theory of intelligent design. Both sides of the debate have well-known scientists and philosophers.

- **Jonathan Wells**—Wells has received two PhDs, one in molecular and cell biology from the University of California at Berkeley and one in religious studies from Yale University. Wells is the author of *Charles Hodge's Critique of Darwinism* and *Icons of Evolution: Science or Myth? Why Much of What We Teach About Evolution Is Wrong*. Currently, he is working on a book criticizing the overemphasis on genes in biology and medicine.

What Americans Really Believe

Since 1859, when Darwin introduced the theory of evolution, it has been a hard idea to sell to Americans. In fact, a November 2004 poll conducted by CBS News confirmed just that. It revealed that overall, the vast majority of Americans still do not believe that humans evolved without direction from a supernatural power: Fifty-five percent think that God created human beings in their present form, and 27 percent say that even if humans evolved, God guided the process. Only 13 percent of Americans say that God was not involved in the process of evolution.[18]

Even more interesting is the way beliefs relate to political affiliation. Only 47 percent of those who voted for John Kerry for president in 2004 say that God created humans as they are now, compared with 67 percent of those who voted for George W. Bush.[19]

The poll also found that most Americans, despite their beliefs about evolution, would not substitute creationism for evolution in public schools. However, about two-thirds of Americans do want creationism taught alongside evolution.[20]

Similarly, a survey conducted in 2005 by the Pew Research Center for the People and the Press found that most Americans—64 percent—are open to the idea of teaching creationism along with evolution in public schools.[21]

"Support for teaching creationism along with evolution is

What Is Evolution?

In general, evolution is a process of change over time. The word evolution is used to mean various types of change. Many different things are said to "evolve" over time, including everything from ideas to fashion. Most commonly, though, the term evolution is used to describe how life on Earth could have been formed and developed. This idea that all living things evolved from simple organisms through a series of natural processes is known as the theory of evolution. It was first developed by a British naturalist, Charles Darwin, who wrote a book in 1859 about the origin of species. Sometimes the term *Darwinism* is used when discussing Darwin's ideas about evolution.

What Is Intelligent Design?

In general, the goal of the intelligent design theory is to explain the sheer complexity of living things. This concept says that certain features of both the universe and of living things are best explained by an intelligent cause rather than by undirected process such as natural selection. Supporters believe that intelligent design is a scientific theory that stands on equal footing with other current theories about the origin of life.

What Is a Theory?

According to the National Academy of Sciences, a theory is a well-substantiated explanation of the natural world. It can include facts, laws, inferences, and tested hypotheses. Theories are supported by evidence and can be tested. You also can use them to make predictions.[22]

A theory is not the same as a hypothesis or a law. For example, a hypothesis is an educated guess about the outcome of an experiment or an observation. A law is a statement of fact that is accepted to be true. An example of a law is the law of gravity.

quite broad-based, with majority support even among [non-Christians], liberal Democrats and those who accept natural selection," the researchers noted.[23]

Finally, almost all Americans believe in God or some higher power, according to a CBS News poll conducted in April 2006. In fact, 82 percent said they believe in God, while 9 percent said they believe in a higher power. It was the younger respondents who expressed the most doubt about the existence of God. Others expressing doubt included those living in the West, political independents, people living in big cities, and men.[24]

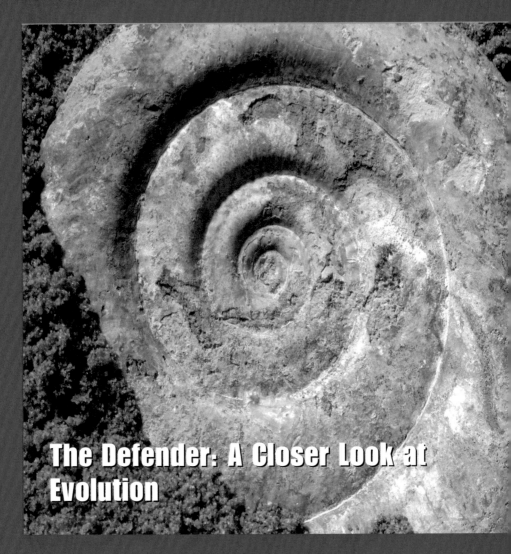

The Defender: A Closer Look at Evolution

The words *evolution* and *Darwinism* are easily recognized by most people. But they are not always understood. Both words cause a lot of misunderstanding, and they are often misused in discussions and debates. Even most students beginning college biology do not fully understand the theory of evolution.

According to the National Association of Biology Teachers (NABT), life on Earth is diverse because of evolution. They define evolution as an "unpredictable and natural process of descent with modification."[1] In addition, the process of evolution consists of both small-scale change and large-scale change. Small-scale change (also called microevolution) is change in a population from one generation to the next. Large-scale change (also called macroevolution) is the descent of different species from a common ancestor over many generations. In other words, evolution says all life on Earth came from and shares a common ancestor.

"Through the process of descent with modification, the common ancestor of life on Earth gave rise to the fantastic diversity that we see documented in the fossil record and around us today," say the authors of *Understanding Evolution*, an educational Web site dedicated to teaching evolutionary biology sponsored by the University of California at Berkeley. "Evolution means that we're all distant cousins: humans and oak trees, hummingbirds and whales."[2]

What's more, evolution only occurs when there is a change in a population over time. These genetic differences are heritable—that is, they can be passed on from parents to offspring. These changes are affected by mutation, genetic drift, natural selection, and other natural forces.

Evolution's Main Ideas

Overall, the theory of evolution consists of several interrelated ideas. The two main ideas are:

1. all species evolved from a single life-form that lived billions of years ago;

2. this process takes place through the interaction of natural forces including, among other things, natural selection, mutation, and genetic drift.

Scientists who accept the theory of evolution believe that the concept of a single life-form evolving describes *what* happened years ago. The idea that natural forces interacted, causing this single life-form to become many life-forms, describes *how* it happened. Following is a closer look at the natural forces involved with evolutionary theory.

Mutation. Mutation is a change in DNA, the hereditary material of life. An organism's DNA affects all aspects of its life, including how it looks and how it acts. According to the Understanding Evolution Web site:

> Mutations can be beneficial, neutral, or harmful for the organism, but mutations do not "try" to supply what the organism "needs." In this respect, mutations are random—whether a particular mutation happens or not is unrelated to how useful that mutation would be.[3]

Mutations happen for several reasons. One reason is that the DNA fails to copy accurately. For example, when a cell divides, it makes a copy of its DNA. Sometimes the copy is not quite perfect. That small difference from the original DNA sequence is called a mutation. Sickle-cell anemia, which is a painful genetic disease, is an example of a mutation. A mutated version of the gene that helps make hemoglobin causes the disease. (Hemoglobin is a protein that carries oxygen in red blood cells.) People with two copies of this sickle-cell gene have the disease, while a person with only one gene will be a carrier.

Exposure to specific chemicals or radiation also can cause mutations. These agents cause the DNA to break down; when the cell repairs the DNA, it might not do a perfect job. Consequently, the cell ends up with DNA slightly different from the original DNA. The result is a mutation.

Genetic drift. Genetic drift is another of the basic mechanisms of evolution. It affects the genetic makeup of the population through an entirely random process. In each generation, due to chance, some living things may leave behind a few more descendents than other living things. These living things inherit some of the genes of the previous generation, regardless of their benefit or purpose. This result is known as genetic drift. It happens to all populations.[4]

Natural selection. Natural selection is said to be the primary way in which these evolutionary changes happen. The idea of natural selection was first introduced by Darwin. When people use the terms *Darwinism* or *Darwinian evolution,* they are most likely referring to Charles Darwin's theory of evolution through natural selection.

Strictly speaking, Darwinism refers only to natural selection and not to evolution in general. Sometimes biologists debate over the accuracy of Darwinism. But when they do, they are not questioning whether or not evolution is true. They are debating about how much natural selection can account for evolutionary change.[5]

According to Darwinism, plants and animals change over time through the process called natural selection. Here is how Darwin said it works:

- Offspring are born that are slightly different from their parents.

- More offspring are born than can survive. Most often the young with features best suited for the environment survive. What's more, the fittest contribute more offspring to the next generation.

- The plants and animals that live then breed and pass on the useful features to their young.

- Over time, these tiny variations in features result in species change. (The word species is used in science to describe different plants and animals belonging to a group. These plants and animals can breed with one other to produce offspring but cannot breed with the members of other groups.)

- The species best adapted to the environment do well; the ones that are poorly adapted die out.[6]

Before his death, Darwin offered another controversial idea about the origin of species. In 1871, he published his most daring book, *The Descent of Man and Selection in Relation to Sex.*

A statue of Charles Darwin. His book *On the Origin of Species by Means of Natural Selection*, published in 1859, transformed science.

The book's purpose was to bring together evidence that humans, like all other species, had evolved from earlier forms that are now extinct. Something is extinct if it has disappeared. Dinosaurs are an example of extinction.

In his book, Darwin suggested that humans are descended from, or are related to, an apelike ancestor. This idea bothered many people. They felt this aspect of evolution—that man and ape are related—was an insult to humankind and a denial of God's gift to humans.

Today, scientists believe that through natural selection, living things that are well adapted to the environment have an advantage over those who are not so well adapted. In other words, they survive longer and reproduce more successfully. The inherited traits that increase survival are then passed to their offspring, giving them the same advantages.

One example of this can be seen by observing populations of beetles in which some are brown and some are green. Because the green beetles are shiny and attract attention, they are eaten more frequently by birds. This leaves more brown beetles left in the population. Brown beetles then pass on the more advantageous trait—brown coloration—to their offspring. As a result, the population will eventually have more brown beetles than green.

The History of Evolution

Ancient Greek philosophers first began discussing the idea of evolution long ago. Throughout the years, various thinkers, philosophers, and scientists would sometimes touch on the subject, but did not get much attention for their ideas. Although Darwin's ideas are considered a breakthrough, there were several earlier contributors to the theory of evolution. These include:

- French philosopher and scientist Charles Bonnet, who created a chart in 1764 showing evolutionary

A Closer Look at Charles Darwin

Charles Robert Darwin (1809–1882) began his career as a failure. Originally, he had hoped to enter the medical field. But when he could not tolerate cutting up dead bodies or participating in surgery, he dropped out.

He then began studying to become a priest in the Church of England. Soon his interest shifted from studying theology to shooting birds, collecting rare beetles, and reading about politics and philosophy.

In 1831, he accepted a position as a naturalist on the *Beagle*, a small ship set to sail around the world. Throughout the voyage, Darwin saw things and collected specimens that kept him busy thinking and writing for the next fifty years.

During his middle-age years, Darwin quietly rejected Christianity. Later, he described himself as agnostic. He continued to believe in a distant, impersonal God who had set the universe and its laws into motion. But he did not believe in a personal God who favored people over other species.[7]

Darwin spent much of his time alone thinking, reading, and studying. Finally, he began writing a book explaining his theory of natural selection. He hurried to complete his book after learning that another scientist, Alfred Wallace, was developing similar ideas. Darwin's book, *On the Origin of Species by Means of Natural Selection*, was published in 1859. All the copies were sold in the very first day.

By the time Darwin died, he was Britain's most respected scientist. Not only did his ideas change the way scientists look at the world, but they also impacted scientific study, especially in the areas of genetics and microbiology.

connections. Bonnet's chart showed human beings at the top and mold at the bottom.

- Swedish botanist and explorer Carolus Linnaeus (1707–1778), who developed a classification system that grouped animals into categories. His classification system showed how different breeds of animals mated and produced creatures of mixed breeds.

- French naturalist Georges Buffon (1707–1788), who developed a theory stating that by looking at species today, its lineage (or family tree) can be traced back to an ancestral starting point. This starting point was one species from which all others evolved. An example would be an ancient feline that developed into the lions, tigers, and housecats we have today.

- The former French army officer Jean-Baptiste Lamarck (1744–1829), who later studied medicine and botany, stated in 1801 that a change in the environment causes the needs of organisms living in that environment to change. This change, he said, then causes a change in behavior that would ultimately lead to a change in whether or not a structure or organ was used or not. Eventually, disuse would cause the structure or organ to shrink or even disappear.

- Darwin's grandfather, Erasmus Darwin (1731–1802), had a theory about evolution. In his book *Zoonomia* (1796), he combined creationism and evolution. He suggested that God designed life but also designed it to be self-improving. He said animals were meant to grow and to adapt to their surroundings.

- The geologist Charles Lyell (1797–1875) published a book where he proposed that changes in the earth's landscape had happened over many, many years. In other words, mountains had slowly grown and coastlines had gradually shifted.

One thing Darwin could never figure out was how features are passed on from parents to offspring. While Darwin was working on his book *Origin of Species*, Gregor Mendel, an Austrian monk, was studying peas and how features are passed on from generation to generation.

One of the features he was experimenting with was color.

Jean-Baptiste Lamarck, a French scientist, proposed a theory of evolution that influenced Darwin's ideas.

Mendel crossed plants that produced yellow peas with plants that produced green peas. What he discovered is that the color of peas is determined by two pieces of information passed on by the two parents. Depending on what the parents passed on would determine the color of peas. But it wasn't until around 1900 that the importance of his work was recognized. Mendel's studies of how features are passed on to other generations are known today as the science of genetics. This field of study is still one of the hottest areas of science.

As a result of Mendel's studies, the current understanding of how evolution works differs considerably from Darwin's original theory. In fact, in the 1930s, scientists combined (or synthesized) Darwin's idea of natural selection with Mendel's theory about heredity to create what is called modern evolutionary synthesis (or sometimes called modern synthesis). Modern synthesis says that natural selection, mutation, genetic drift, and other natural forces cause the changes in populations over time. This theory

> **Today, scientists believe that through natural selection, living things that are well adapted to the environment have an advantage over those that are not so well adapted.**

has become the cornerstone of biology. It helps scientists understand a variety of topics, including things like bacteria's resistance to antibiotics and insects' resistance to pesticides.

However, the creation of the synthetic theory did not lead to agreement on all the details of evolution. For example, some scientists still disagree on how big a part natural selection and genetic drift play in evolution. This and other controversies with the theory still continue.

The Theory of Evolution Today

The theory of evolution is considered by many scientists to be one of the most important concepts in biology. It is used to explain a number of things in science.

Social Darwinism

Although Darwin did not apply his theory to human society, later thinkers used his ideas to explain why people in society are not all the same. For example, in the mid-1860s, Herbert Spencer made up the phrase "survival of the fittest."

Since then, people have used the theory to suggest that human society is a battleground in which only the strongest or best survive. This idea is called social Darwinism.

According to this theory, people compete to survive, and the fittest become richer and own more property. Additionally, the theory suggests that poverty proves weakness. Many people do not agree with social Darwinism because it does not consider other contributing factors, such as family background and historical events.

What's more, social Darwinism is believed to have led to the racist policies of groups such as the Nazis. In the 1930s in Germany, the Nazi Party came into power; over the next decade, Nazis killed millions of people. They claimed to be protecting the world from Jews, Gypsies, Slavs, and other "inferior" people.

Eugenics was another controversial idea that had its roots in Darwin's theory. According to those who believe in eugenics, people who are genetically superior (indicated by their being successful and healthy) should be encouraged to reproduce, while the genetically inferior (indicated by such factors as poverty and poor health) should be prevented from reproducing.

For example, understanding evolution can make a big difference in how diseases are treated. Although the evolution of disease-causing organisms may move faster than the invention of new treatments, studying the evolution of drug resistance may help slow it. Additionally, learning about the origins of diseases may provide clues as to how to treat them. And finally, considering the basic processes of evolution may bring understanding about the roots of genetic diseases.

However, because evolutionary theory also states that humans evolved from a single life-form and that they share a common ancestor with apes, it is still a very controversial idea. Opponents argue that ideas such as natural selection and random mutation cannot account for the complexity of life.

In 2001, a group of spokespersons for the Public Broadcasting System's (PBS) seven-part television series *Evolution* issued a statement saying that "all known scientific evidence supports [Darwinian] evolution," as does "virtually

Materialistic Evolution

Critics of evolution often worry that young students are being taught not just evolution in biology class but also a philosophy based on evolution known as "materialistic evolution." Materialistic evolution implies that material, or matter, is all there is. (Materialistic evolution is sometimes called naturalistic evolution when it implies that nature is all there is.)

In other words, materialistic (or naturalistic) evolution teaches students that with evolution there is no need for a supernatural intelligence or any intelligent design. There is no need for God. Famous evolutionist George Gaylord Simpson supports this view, saying, "Man is the result of a purposeless and natural process that did not have him in mind."[8]

What's more, Lewis Menand, a scholar of American intellectual history, says what was radical about Darwin's theory of evolution by natural selection was not the idea itself, but his materialism. "Darwin wanted to establish . . . that the species—including humans—were created by, and evolve according to, processes that are entirely natural, chance-generated and blind."[9]

Consequently, critics maintain that teaching evolution from this perspective means that people's lives have no higher purpose. They also argue that looking at evolution this way goes beyond the boundaries of science and becomes more about religion and philosophy.

"If nature is all there is then nature had to have the ability to do its own creating," explains Philip Johnson, one of the initiators of the ID movement. "Darwinian evolution is a theory about how nature might have done this, without assistance from a supernatural Creator. That is why (Darwinian evolution) is by definition mindless and godless."[10]

every reputable scientist in the world." In reply, a group of one hundred scientists, researchers, and professors made it known that this was not the case.[11]

Among those protesting were well respected, world-class scientists, including Henry F. Schaefer, a frequently cited chemist; James Tour of Rice University's Center for Nanoscale Science and Technology; and Fred Figworth, professor of cellular and molecular physiology at Yale Graduate School.[12]

They ran a two-page advertisement in a national magazine with the title "A Scientific Dissent from Darwinism." Their statements were direct and to the point. "We are skeptical of claims for the ability of random mutation and natural selection to account for the complexity of life," they said. "Careful examination of the evidence for Darwinian theory should be encouraged."[13]

Eugenie C. Scott, executive director for the National Center for Science Education, responded that it was of no surprise that there was a backlash over the PBS series: "Although virtually every reputable scientist in the world agrees that evolution is good science, some people still refuse to accept it … [because it is] incompatible with their religious beliefs."[14]

The Challenger: A Closer Look at Intelligent Design

Unlike Darwinism, which suggests that natural causes are solely responsible for the development of life, the intelligent design theory takes a different approach in explaining life.

In general, ID theory states that certain features of the natural world are so complex that the most likely explanation is that they are the result of an intelligent cause. Because of this complexity, supporters do not believe random mutation and natural selection alone could have caused these features.

Certain systems in nature just cannot be explained by evolution, they say. Such systems have the mark of an intelligent agent. "The justification for design is that these systems seem to have features we associate with designed systems," says Michael Behe, a Lehigh University biologist and author of *Darwin's Black Box*. "They have intricate parts that interact with each other."[1]

Until these "parts" are proven to result from evolution, Behe says, scientists should allow for the idea that they were intelligently designed.[2] In fact, Behe asserts, more and more scientists are starting to agree with this line of thinking. The number of scientists who have signed the "Scientific Dissent from Darwinism" now stands at more than five hundred.[3]

Finally, intelligent design supporters maintain that their theory is not the same as creationism. Although supporters do not believe the natural world happened by chance, the "designer" could be anyone or anything.

The History of Intelligent Design

Design theory, which says that nature shows real signs of having been designed by an intelligent agent, is not a new concept. In fact, the design argument has been around since ancient Greece.

The most famous argument for design was developed by theologian William Paley. In 1802, Paley suggested that things in nature were so perfectly designed for their roles in life that they could not possibly have come into being by themselves. There had to have been a creator.

Paley used an example of a watchmaker to illustrate his point. While walking, suppose you tripped over a stone and you asked, "How did that stone come to be there?" You might answer, "It has been there forever." But what if you found a watch on the ground and you asked the same question? The answer given for the stone ("it has been there forever") would not be sufficient to explain the watch.

"The watch must have had a maker ... who comprehended its construction, and designed its use," Paley explains.[4]

Is Intelligent Design Really Creationism in Disguise?

Generally speaking, creationism is a set of beliefs based on the idea that a Supreme Being (usually called God) brought all of life on Earth into existence through a direct act of creation. The story of creation is told in Genesis, the first book of the Bible.

Creationism comes in many varieties. The strictest form adheres to a literal interpretation of the Bible and believes that Earth is only a few thousand years old. At the other end of the spectrum is the idea of theistic evolutionism. This view accepts evidence that Earth is billions of years old and that evolution can explain much of its history—but not the creation of the human soul. There are also Young Earth and Old Earth creationists. These two groups disagree over the age of the earth and the specifics of how God created life.[5]

Since its development, opponents of intelligent design have tried to portray the theory as another form of creationism. Although it is compatible with many creationist views, it also is very different. Unlike creationism, which points toward God, intelligent design says only that there are intelligent causes for life's complexity and that these causes can be detected.

For this reason, intelligent design has been criticized for encouraging a loose reading of the Bible. Creationists also worry that this theory minimizes God. For example, Reasons to Believe, a creationist group that accepts Earth is billions of years old, says that intelligent design is not science. Meanwhile, the Institute for Creation Research, which maintains a literal six-day interpretation of Genesis, says intelligent design is not biblical. What's more, many creationist scholars do not want to require public schools to teach intelligent design. But they want students to be taught both the strengths and weaknesses of evolution.[6]

Still, despite the differences in beliefs, the goal of both intelligent design supporters and creationists is the same. They both want to dislodge what they see as evolutionist dogma from science classrooms. (Dogma is a set of beliefs that a particular group holds to be true.)[7]

Paley argued that we could draw the same conclusions about many natural objects. One example is the eye. The eye's parts make it perfect for seeing just like a watch's parts are perfect for telling time. He says that in both an eye and a watch we can see it took an intelligent designer.[8]

Paley's ideas influenced thinkers for decades. But because he never provided a way to detect design in nature, his idea was an easy target for Darwinism. As Darwinism took root, design theory was rejected in biology.[9]

Yet despite attempts to push intelligent design aside, there were always people who thought Darwin's theory was inadequate. These scholars were not convinced that "undirected natural causes" could produce the diversity and complexity of life.

It was not until the 1980s that these thinkers became more organized. This new wave of scientists and thinkers were convinced that Darwin's theory could not explain the complexity of living things.[10]

In 1991, Phillip Johnson, sometimes referred to as the father of the modern intelligent design movement, popularized the idea of intelligent design in his book *Darwin on Trial.* Additionally, Johnson has been instrumental in developing a number of strategies for promoting intelligent design.

Overall, the difference between intelligent design today and intelligent design of years ago is that today's theory does not try to infer God's existence. Instead, it claims only that intelligent causes are necessary to explain the complex structures of biology. What's more, intelligent design states that these causes can be detected.[11]

Intelligent Design's Main Ideas

In his best-known book, *On the Origin of Species by Means of Natural Selection* (often referred to as *Origin of Species*), Darwin wrote: "If it could be demonstrated that any complex organ

A Closer Look at the Creationists' Clash With Evolution

Public high schools in the United States began teaching evolution in science classes in the early 1900s. By the 1920s, creationists had proposed laws in twenty states banning public schools from teaching evolution. Several states, including Tennessee and Arkansas, passed the suggested legislation.

The American Civil Liberties Union (ACLU) believed that this new legislation violated the constitution. In 1925, the ACLU challenged the new law in Tennessee through the Scopes trial. Although the ACLU lost the case, creationism suffered as a result of the trial. The media portrayed creationists as uninformed, religious zealots.

In 1968, the Supreme Court of the United States ruled that banning the teaching of evolution in the school was unconstitutional. Despite this setback, creationism gained support in the 1960s. By the 1970s and 1980s, scientific creationists proposed laws that would have made creationism a required subject in classrooms that taught evolution. In 1981, Arkansas and Louisiana passed the suggested laws. But by 1987, the courts ruled that creationism was a religion and teaching it would be unconstitutional. They also said that evolution was a science and could be taught in public schools.

In response to these court rulings, creationists shifted their focus to political activities in local school districts and communities. Their focus has been to demonstrate how the teaching of evolution in classrooms should be altered. One common complaint is that the theory of evolution is taught as an undisputed fact and the holes within the theory are not fully discussed.

existed which could not possibly have been formed by numerous, successive, slight modifications, my theory would absolutely break down."[12]

This is exactly what intelligent design theorists claim they have done—identified complex organs or features that could not have been formed through numerous slight changes over time. As a result, they believe that Darwinism is "absolutely breaking down" as Darwin himself suggested it might.

Overall, the intelligent design theory contains several key concepts, including:

1. irreducible complexity

2. specified complexity

3. information mechanisms

4. fine-tuned universe

According to supporters of intelligent design, these concepts, as well as several other ideas, prove that the complexities of life could not have occurred by chance, as Darwin claimed. They also cast doubt on a naturalistic approach to evolution, which implies that nature is all there is.

Simply put, intelligent design theorists point to evidence or signs of intelligence. These signs are physical attributes that they say require design and could not have occurred by chance.

Irreducible complexity. Michael Behe coined the phrase "irreducible complexity." By definition, if something is irreducibly complex, this means it has several interacting parts that help it to do its job. If one of the parts is removed, then it no longer functions.[13]

When something is irreducibly complex, any system that came before it would not be able to function because one or more of the parts would be missing. Therefore, an irreducibly complex system could not have been produced by the numerous slight changes over time that are said to occur with natural selection.[14]

Behe illustrates irreducible complexity by using a mousetrap as an example. Mousetraps contain a number of parts, including:

1. a flat wooden platform to act as a base

2. a metal hammer, which traps the mouse

Michael Behe, a professor of bio-chemistry at Lehigh University and one of the best known supporters of intelligent design, coined the phrase "irreducible complexity."

3. a wire spring with extended ends to press against the platform and the hammer

4. a sensitive catch, which releases when pressure is applied

5. a metal bar, which holds the hammer back

6. assorted staples and screws to hold the system together

If any of the mousetrap's parts are removed, then the trap will not work. In other words, the mousetrap cannot trap a mouse until all the parts are assembled. The same is true of many things in biology, Behe says. If one of the parts is removed, it will not work. (Behe's argument has been assailed by Kenneth Miller, who has a mousetrap with one of its parts removed and the remaining parts bent so that the mechanism still traps mice. He wears the contraption as a tie clip.[15])

Behe gives several examples of irreducibly complex items in biology, including eyesight, the mechanism for clotting blood, cilia (threadlike structures on cells), and bacterial flagellum. The last is one of the more popular examples.

In simple terms, the flagellum is a swimming device for bacteria. It provides a way for bacteria to move around very quickly. More specifically, the flagellum is a long hairlike filament embedded in the cell membrane. If this filament or flagellum is broken off, it floats stiffly in the water. It does not function on its own. Its purpose is to propel the bacteria, but without the rest of the bacteria, it does not do anything. As a result, Behe makes the argument that the bacteria flagellum needs all its parts to work.[16]

In his book, Behe writes that the bacterial flagellum is composed of three main parts. These parts resemble a paddle, a rotor, and a motor—much like the outboard motor of a boat. The idea that all three parts could assemble into a working "motor" is hard to imagine without the help of an intelligent designer—especially since natural selection "selects" only the traits best for survival.

> **Today, intelligent design theory does not try to infer God's existence. Instead, it claims only that intelligent causes are necessary to explain the complex structures of biology.**

This flagellum example is the basis of the argument of irreducible complexity, which says that an unintelligent source like nature would not know to "select" the flagellum in a preexisting organism. To nature, the flagellum would seem unnecessary because it does not work alone.

Specified complexity. In general, specified complexity is a method used to determine whether or not something is the result of an intelligent agent. An object or event displays specified complexity when the odds are extremely low that the object or event happened by chance. The object or event also matches a recognizable pattern. According to intelligent design theory, when you see specified complexity, you can use that as a sign of an intelligent agent.[17]

This aspect of intelligent design is what makes it different from earlier versions, says William Dembski, author of *No Free Lunch*. Instead of looking for an object's purpose or looking for perfection as in the past, ID scientists look for specified complexity. If something is specified, that means it fits a recognizable pattern. If something is complex, that means there are so many ways the object could have turned out that the chance of getting that exact object (without an intelligent agent) is very small.[18]

Information mechanisms. Our bodies contain one hundred trillion cells, and each cell contains six feet of DNA. This DNA contains a four-letter chemical alphabet that spells out exact instructions for all the proteins that make up the human body. Stephen Meyer, author of *Darwinism, Design and Public Education*, asserts that no hypothesis has come close to explaining how information like this got into organisms through natural selection.[19]

In fact, Meyer says an orderly arrangement that is both complex and has a specific pattern or function is always the product of intelligence. Books and computer codes are examples from everyday life.[20]

Professor Michael Behe uses a mousetrap as an illustration of the concept of irreducible complexity in everyday life.

DNA also has these two properties—it is complex, and it corresponds to an independent pattern or function. Meyer says that the presence of this type of information in DNA points toward an intelligent source. The Cambrian period of the fossil record is another example of information pointing toward an intelligent source. This period contains an impressive group of life-forms. He says massive amounts of biological information would have been required, because all the fossils appeared fully formed.[21]

"Information is the hallmark of mind," says Meyer. "And purely from the evidence of genetics and biology, we can infer the existence of a mind that's far greater than our own—a conscious, purposeful, rational, intelligent designer who's amazingly creative."[22]

Fine-tuned universe. Intelligent design supporters argue that we live in a fine-tuned universe, which contains many features that make life possible. But, they add, these features cannot be attributed to chance. They include things such as the values of physical constants, the strength of nuclear forces, chemical processes, and many other features that work together with amazing efficiency. Supporters say that if any of these values were even slightly different, the universe would be dramatically different.

For example, according to astronomer Guillermo Gonzalez and science philosopher Jay W. Richards, authors of the book *The Privileged Planet,* "It would take a star with the highly unusual properties of our sun—the right mass, the right light, the right age, the right distance, the right orbit, the right galaxy, the right location—to nurture living organisms on a circling planet." Moreover, there are numerous factors that make both our solar system and Earth's location a safe place for humans to live.[23]

"If the universe had not been made with the most exacting precision we could never have come into existence," says John

A. O'Keefe of NASA, a Harvard-educated astrophysicist. "It is my view that these circumstances indicate the universe was created for man to live in."[24]

Intelligent Design Theory Today

The intelligent design movement began with a number of scholars critiquing Darwinism on both scientific and philosophical grounds. On scientific grounds, they felt Darwinism was not an adequate explanation for biology. On philosophical grounds, they felt it represented naturalism, the view that nature is all that is needed. With naturalism, there is no need for God or any guiding intelligence.[25]

For years, there were no methods for determining if objects were made by an intelligent force or by a natural force. Consequently, the intelligent design theory was not part of mainstream science for more than 130 years. But in the last five years, intelligent design has exploded. Scholars who support ID have proposed a research program where intelligent causes become the key to understanding the diversity and complexity of life.[26]

Scientists who endorse intelligent design use research methods found in other sciences, such as forensic science, archeology, and the search for extraterrestrial life.[27]

"[Intelligent design] is responsible for Darwinism losing its corner on the intellectual market," explains Dembski. "If fully successful, intelligent design will unseat not just Darwinism but also Darwinism's cultural legacy."[28]

Moreover, intelligent design does not suggest there is a divine creator or miracles. It simply detects intelligence without discussing who or what that intelligence is. In fact, intelligent design theory today has such a narrow definition that it is compatible with a wide range of views. For example, some intelligent design supporters believe in some aspects of evolution.

And there are other supporters of intelligent design theory who believe in a literal reading of the creation story in the book of Genesis in the Bible.[29]

According to William Dembski, "For intelligent design, the first question is not how organisms came to be . . . but whether they demonstrate clear . . . detectable marks of being intelligently caused."[30]

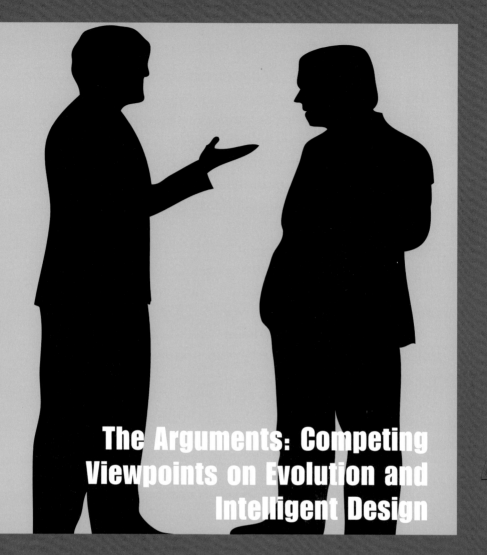

The Arguments: Competing Viewpoints on Evolution and Intelligent Design

Charles Darwin liked to describe his book *Origin of Species* as "one long argument."[1] But his explanation of evolution now seems brief compared to the argument that has followed in its wake. More than 150 years after his book was published the argument continues. Today, the debate revolves around ideas and facts, the meaning of science, and the role of faith. Never in the history of science has one theory been so fiercely debated. And the end is nowhere in sight.

"It is an emotional topic," says Gerry Wheeler, executive director of the National Science Teachers Association. "If we have any ounce of spirituality in us, these are high-stakes questions and we have to honor everybody on the spectrum of the debate."[2]

To the average American, the debate over evolution and intelligent design can appear very tangled. Combine that with misinformation and heated emotions and the debate gets even more muddled. Ultimately, both sides spend a large amount of time, energy, and money trying to prove their points and to discredit their opponents.

Generally speaking, supporters of intelligent design want the evidence they say discredits some of evolutionary thinking to be taught in America's science classrooms. They call this approach "teaching the controversy." They also want teachers and students to have the academic freedom to discuss the issue openly and critically, considering all options and ideas for the origin of species.

Evolutionists, on the other hand, say, "What controversy?" They counter their opponents' arguments by saying that intelligent design is simply a pseudoscience. Instead, they say both the "teach the controversy" approach and claims about an intelligent designer are nothing more than a political attempt to get creationism back in the classroom.

Redesigning Evolution Teaching: The Intelligent Design Perspective

The biggest complaint for intelligent design supporters is how evolution is taught in classrooms across the country. From their perspective, schools are rigid in their teaching of evolution. They claim students are taught that the material, or natural, world is all there is—that there is only one logical explanation for how life on Earth came to be.

Instead, intelligent design supporters want educators to teach students how to think and ask questions about evolution rather than just blindly accepting what is presented. Erica Van Dop agrees.

She says, "Even if other scientists believe that evolution is contradictory to intelligent design, it is a theory that is being talked about. So whether it is valid or not, kids should be educated on all sides so they can make their own decision."[3]

Moreover, from an intelligent design perspective, the debate is not really about evolution as a whole. Instead, the focus is very narrow. As ID supporters see it, the debate is really about Darwinism, or more specifically, neo-Darwinism. Neo-Darwinism is the modern approach to Darwin's original theory; it says that favorable variations occur by both natural selection and random mutations.

Interestingly, the vast majority of intelligent design supporters accept many components of evolution. For example, intelligent design supporters accept that the earth is billions of years old and that life has evolved. They even accept some common ancestry. What they do not accept is that *all* life evolved from a single organism.

What's more, intelligent design supporters do not want to ban the teaching of evolution in public schools. In fact, they often advocate that evolution be taught. They also do not support mandatory teaching of intelligent design as an alternative to evolution. But, what they do want is a more careful presentation of evolutionary theory including information and ideas that scientists are arguing about.[4]

Jonathan Wells, the author of *Icons of Evolution* and a supporter of intelligent design theory, says that Darwinists often respond to critics by saying evolution simply means change over time. But he feels this response skirts around the truth.

"No rational person denies the reality of change. . . . If 'evolution' meant only this it would be utterly uncontroversial," he says.[5]

No one doubts that descent with modification occurs either, he says. "We see this in our own families, and plant and animal breeders see it in their work." Like change over time,

Wells says, descent with modification within a species is utterly uncontroversial.[6]

"But Darwinian evolution claims much more," Wells says. "In particular, it claims that descent with modification explains the origin and diversification of all living things."[7]

According to author Jonathan Wells, "No rational person denies the reality of change. . . . If 'evolution' meant only this it would be utterly uncontroversial."

Intelligent design supporters also point to controversies surrounding evolution. They want these controversies taught in the classroom. Some of the controversies involve the fossil record, a 1953 simulation of the earth's early atmosphere, drawings of apelike creatures evolving into humans, and early embryos.

"If you ask almost any scientist to describe the evidence for Darwinism, time after time they give these same examples," says Wells. "They're in our textbooks. They're what we teach our students. For many scientists they *are* the evidence."[8]

Darwinian evolution must be continually compared with the evidence, like all other scientific theories, says Wells. "If it does not fit the evidence, it must be reevaluated or abandoned—otherwise it is not science, but myth," he says.[9]

Evolving Attacks: The Evolution Perspective

Evolution supporters say there is no controversy. From their perspective, the emergence of the intelligent design debate is just another attempt to undermine evolutionary thinking and teaching. They also say that creation has evolved into intelligent design theory. As a result, they believe the theory is really just a religious view.

Evolutionists also say that the theory of intelligent design is not science—it is instead a pseudoscience. And the push to critically analyze evolution in science classrooms is nothing more than a political ploy to get creationism back into the classroom.

In fact, evolutionists say that intelligent design supporters do not have an established research program and have published no data in respected scientific journals to support their claims. What's more, they say that the intelligent design theory provides supernatural answers to scientific questions, so that it simply does not meet the definition of science.

"Intelligent design fails not because the scientific community is closed to [the idea. ID fails] rather for the most basic of reasons—because it is overwhelmingly contradicted by the scientific evidence," says Kenneth Miller, an evolutionist and author of *Finding Darwin's God*.[10]

Evolutionists also assert that the theory cannot be seriously disputed and that it is the cornerstone of biology. They also say it is widely accepted by the majority of scientists. They do admit that scientists debate things like how much natural selection accounts for change. But they argue that no reputable scientist feels the theory is false.

"Sometimes [a scientist's] work has changed our understanding of significant details of how evolution operates, but the theory of evolution still has essentially unanimous agreement from the people who work on it," explains Mark Isaak of the Talk Origins Web site and author of *The Counter-Creationism Handbook*.[11]

Kenneth Miller, a professor of biology at Brown University, is a notable supporter of evolutionary theory who says that intelligent design is contradicted by the scientific evidence.

Finally, supporters of evolution point out that the intelligent design movement has a very aggressive public relations program. This program, they say, includes conferences, popular books and articles, lectures on college campuses to recruit students, and alliances with conservative Christians and influential political figures.

"[The intelligent design movement] is advancing," says Barbara Forrest, an associate professor of philosophy at Southeastern Louisiana University and a supporter of evolution, "but its tactics are no substitute for real science."[12]

A Closer Look at the Main Arguments

There are numerous points argued within the evolution versus intelligent design debate. But today, the two sides seem to be squaring off over the "controversial" aspects of evolutionary theory.

Intelligent design supporters say there is evidence that casts doubt on Darwinism. Evolutionists say that these points are not really in dispute nor do they cast doubt on the theory at all. From their point of view, there are logical explanations for each criticism.

Also topping the list is the debate about how life on Earth came to be. Evolutionists say that life resulted from random naturalistic processes, while intelligent design supporters say that life resulted from intelligent purposeful design.

Finally, both sides disagree about what constitutes science, religion, and philosophy, and more importantly, what is appropriate in the classroom.

Intelligent design supporters say there is a controversy surrounding evolution and they want it exposed in science classrooms. They want to ensure that students are given all the facts and are allowed to make decisions on their own. They do not want evolution to have a monopoly in science classrooms. And while they still want evolution taught, they do not want it taught as absolute fact with no room for exploration of other ideas and opinions.

Evolutionists, on the other hand, maintain that there is no controversy. Instead, they say that the intelligent design movement's push to teach the controversy is actually just a ploy to get "creationism" back in science classes.

They argue that the scientific community accepts evolution and there is no need to present challenges to it in the classroom. They feel presenting "challenges" would only confuse students.

The Controversy!

Most intelligent design advocates want evolution taught in schools. What they want to change is *how* it is taught. They also think students should be taught to think about evolution critically and examine the evidence that is put forth.

"We think students should learn [about evolution]," says Casey Luskin, cofounder of the Intelligent Design and Evolution Awareness (IDEA) Center, an online resource for teachers. "It's a very influential theory in modern biology, and students need to understand what it is. What hurts them is if you teach them to just absorb and swallow evolution as uncritical fact."[13]

Competent history teachers normally make arguments about their subject matter readily available to students, says Patrick Groff, a professor at San Diego State University. He feels science teachers should do the same.

"To prohibit science teachers from following [history teachers'] example seems to me an anti-intellectual, unprofessional restriction on their academic freedom," Groff adds.[14]

So what is the controversy intelligent design supporters want to expose? Aside from wanting to expose Darwinism as being a materialistic philosophy, they want "the evidence" for evolution to receive more balance in the classroom. The following are just a few of the many arguments about evidence that they feel should be presented in a more balanced fashion.

The fossil record. Fossils, which are hardened forms of things that were once living, are often used as evidence of evolution. In fact, the National Academy of Sciences' guidebook says that "the fossil record provides powerful evidence for evolution."[15] But intelligent design supporters disagree. They point to inconsistencies in the fossil record, gaps, and even forgeries.

For example, ID supporters say the evidence does not show gradual change like Darwinism suggests. Instead, most fossils appear to have been formed at the same time, without much change from one to the other. Moreover, they say there are gaps in the record. They say what is missing from the fossil record are the many intermediate forms that Darwin said would be found.[16]

Additionally, they say that nearly every major animal group seems to suddenly appear from nowhere—not gradually over time like Darwinism suggests. This period of time is sometimes called the "Cambrian explosion" because so many animals appear all at once.[17]

Finally, intelligent design supporters point out the number of fossil forgeries that have cropped up over the years. They feel this casts doubt on the accuracy of the fossil record. For example, Alan Feduccia, an evolutionary biologist, said that there are scores of fake fossils out there and that fossil forgeries are often sold on the black market.[18]

The 1953 Miller-Urey experiment. The Miller-Urey experiment took place when scientists Stanley Miller and Harold Urey attempted to show how life on Earth could have originated. Miller shot electricity through an atmosphere similar to what early Earth was believed to be like. As a result, molecules such as amino acids were created. These molecules are the building blocks of life.

However, since the 1960s, scientists have shown that the

"atmosphere" Miller selected was not at all like the one scientists believe may have existed. Additionally, in 1995 *Science* magazine said experts now dismiss Miller's experiment.[19]

Yet textbooks still present the experiment as evidence for evolution. Sometimes it is featured prominently in textbooks with pictures. This approach implies that it was the first successful attempt to show how organic molecules might have been produced on early Earth. This can be misleading for students, says Wells. He says that the experiment does not work when conditions are changed to reflect the Earth's early atmosphere.[20]

Drawings of apelike creatures evolving into man. Probably the most famous example of evolution is the drawing of various forms of primates, from the most primitive to modern man, showing the process of evolution, says Wells. "[This drawing] suggests we're merely animals that evolved by purposeless natural causes," he says.[21]

But intelligent design supporters say there is little evidence that supports this drawing. They also say the drawing misrepresents the evidence. In fact, the field of human origins is one of the most fiercely debated topics in biology because of the lack of specific evidence, says Wells.[22]

Instead, he says this idea is based more on materialistic philosophy than it is on the evidence. For example, the apelike fossil man, often called Java man, is based only on speculation of what he should have looked like. What's more, the only things to base this speculation on is a skullcap, a femur (thigh bone), and three teeth.[23]

Embryos. Darwin considered evidence from embryos to be some of the best evidence supporting his theory. Embryos are animals in their earliest stages of development. Biologist Ernst Haeckel first illustrated this evidence in a series of drawings.

In these pictures, the embryos start out looking identical. But, their appearances change as they grow until they look like

A fish fossil. According to the National Academy of Sciences, fossils give powerful evidence for the theory of evolution.

their particular class of animals. The problem is—Haeckel's drawings are fakes.[24]

Scientists have known for years that vertebrate embryos look very different from the beginning. (Vertebrates are animals with a segmented spine and a well-developed brain.) In fact, embryos do not look alike until a few stages later. And then, later in development, they look vastly different again.[25]

Yet, Haeckel's embryos are still found in biology textbooks—as if they were true to life. This fact is one that greatly disturbs intelligent design supporters. They feel evolutionists are teaching kids false information as a way of indoctrinating them about the claims of Darwinism.[26]

Wells says that Darwinists also try to get around the differences in embryos by using the theory to explain why the differences are there.[27]

"But then, *where's the evidence for the theory?*" he asks. "Why should I accept the theory as being true at all?"[28]

What Controversy?

Evolution supporters argue that there is no controversy surrounding evolution in the scientific community. Instead, they say the intelligent design movement has manufactured a controversy as a way to promote their ideas. They also say intelligent design's idea of promoting "critical thinking" has gained momentum because it appeals to the American tradition of balance and fairness.[29]

"Critical thinking is important but you won't promote critical thinking by misinforming students, which is what you do if you pretend that evolution is not scientifically solid," says Nick Matzke of the National Center for Science Education.[30]

Evolutionists believe the public has the false impression that a true scientific controversy exists. They maintain that "intelligent design singles out evolution and misrepresents its status in the scientific community."[31] As a result, they fear students will doubt the soundness of the theory without scientific proof. They also say that only a very small number of scientists support intelligent design.

Finally, they say intelligent design is not just attacking evolution, but it is attacking science. Supporters of evolution are also concerned that intelligent design will threaten the nation's scientific and technological leadership. And they are worried that the politics surrounding the issue will impede the free flow of scientific information.[32]

Supporters of evolution offer the following counterarguments to supporters of intelligent design:

The fossil record. According to evolutionists, fossils are the most easily observed evidence for evolution. The fossil record, they say, represents the pattern of evolution through long spans of time.

Since the 1830s, scientists have noted how fossils became more complex through time. For example, scientists saw that the oldest rocks contained no fossils. Then they found simple sea creatures in rocks followed by more complex fish. After fish, they found life on land occurred, then reptiles, and then mammals. Finally humans came.

Early scientists reasoned that there was some type of "progress" taking place. This progress, they say was explained in 1859 by Darwin. Since then, they say, no fossils have been found that Darwin would not have expected.[33]

As for gaps in the fossil record, evolutionists such as Richard Dawkins say that while gaps exist, they are not really an issue; it is just that not all the evidence has been found yet. Dawkins says that much like detectives, evolutionists have to make inferences from footprints and other types of evidence.[34]

Evolutionists say fossils give us lots of information about things of the past. For example, we can learn about plants and animals that no longer exist. And, we can learn the order in which living things appeared. Fossils also tell a story about how life recovered after major events such as mass extinctions.[35]

Overall, evolutionists maintain that the fossil record is crucial to understanding evolution. And the strict rules involved in testing and dating fossils ensures the accuracy of the fossil record.[36]

The 1953 Miller-Urey experiment. Evolutionists maintain that the Miller-Urey experiment is important. It was the first experiment to show that important molecules could be made from nonliving material using natural processes.

When modern scientists changed the experiment to reflect current knowledge of Earth's early atmosphere, they were able to produce most of the same amino acids that Miller had. The device Miller designed became the basis for later experiments and is still being used today. As a result, evolutionists say that the experiment is a good teaching example because it shows how experimental science works.

"It is also an interesting experiment that is simple enough for most students to grasp," says Alan Gishlick of the National Center for Science Education (NCSE). "[What's more] the basic results are still valid . . . even though research has moved beyond [their work]. We still teach Newton even though we have moved beyond his work."[37]

Finally, the Miller-Urey experiment marks the beginning of experimental research into the origin of life. Therefore, evolutionists say at the very least the experiment is historically important.[38]

Drawings of apelike creatures evolving into man. The NCSE says that these drawings of humans and their ancestors constitute a general outline. Additionally, they maintain that most biologists agree on this issue—even with new discoveries.[39]

"The notion that such drawings are used to 'justify materialistic claims' is ludicrous and not borne out by an examination of textbook treatments of human evolution," says the NCSE.[40]

Embryos. Supporters of evolution maintain that the theory of evolution is not founded on Haeckel's ideas. In fact, they agree that his work has been discredited since the nineteenth century.[41]

However, they also point out that vertebrate embryos do have real similarities. A number of current studies support the idea of similarities, while none question existence of similarities.

Finally, because similarities do exist, evolutionists argue that embryos could be evidence for common descent. For example, they say that even humans, who do not have tails, start out with "tailed" embryos.

How Did Life on Earth Originate?

"Where do we come from?" "How did life on Earth begin?" These are questions that have been asked for years. Some

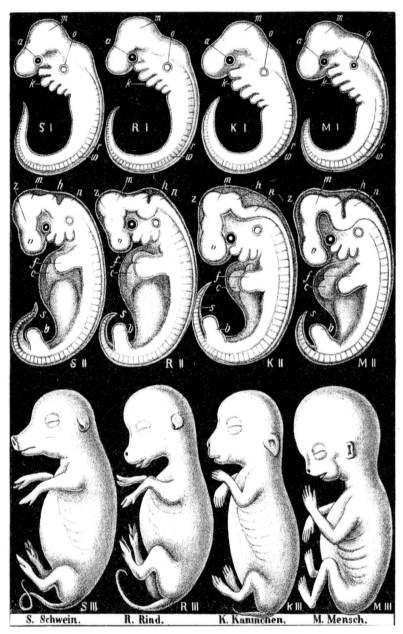

In the nineteenth century, biologist Ernst Haeckel published drawings showing similarities between (left to right) pig, calf, rabbit, and human embryos. However, Haeckel's work in this area has been discredited, and it is not currently used to support the theory of evolution.

people believe that God created all life on Earth; others believe it came to be through natural processes. Still others believe a combination of the two.

The question of how life on Earth originated or began is sometimes called "origins of life." The debate over the origins of life is one of the most fiercely argued points between intelligent design theorists and evolution theorists.

Purposeful, intelligent design. Intelligent design supporters accept some aspects of evolution. For example, they acknowledge that evolution, or change in general, is a fact. They agree with evolutionists that the earth is old. And they agree that the plants and animals around today did not always exist and that some plants and animals that used to exist, such as dinosaurs, are no longer here.

Intelligent design supporters also accept that minor changes in living things still occur today. Some examples of this include mosquitoes becoming resistant to pesticides and bacteria becoming resistant to antibiotics.

What they do not accept is that Darwin's theory of natural selection and random variation accounts for all change—both big and small. And they do not accept that every living thing today originated from a single organism billions of years ago.

The issue, they say, is not whether natural selection can produce minor changes. The issue is whether the process of natural selection can create new tissues, organs, or limbs. They also assert that the data supporting natural selection tells us nothing about the origin of the world, the origin of life, and the development of complex life forms.

So, they propose intelligent design as another theory for the origin of life. They argue that some living things are just too complex to have evolved by chance with no help from a designer. For example, Michael Behe, one of the leading biologists for the intelligent design movement, argues that living organisms contain structures like the eye or mechanisms for clotting blood that could not be products of natural selection. The reason he says is that they are irreducibly complex. And when parts are removed or altered the structure is useless.

Another argument for intelligent design is proposed by William Dembski. Dembski uses math and probability to show that natural selection cannot account for nature's complexity.

What's more, intelligent design supporters maintain that their theory is science and not religion. It makes no claims about whom or what the designer is. Instead, its intellectual roots are the writings of Plato and Aristotle as opposed to Genesis in the Bible. This aspect makes the theory more agnostic rather than creationist.

Finally, intelligent design supporters point out that their focus is very narrow. They are challenging only one part of evolution, and that is Darwinism.

Natural selection and random mutation. Evolutionists believe that natural selection, an idea first proposed by Darwin, is one of the basic mechanisms of evolution. As a result, they argue that populations are able to change in order to best fit their environment. Consequently, natural selection ensures that the organisms most adapted to survive are the most likely to pass on their genes.

Evolutionists agree that the world is filled with complex organisms, just as intelligent design supporters point out. But they argue the evidence supports the trial-and-error mechanism of natural selection.[42]

Conversely, supporters of evolution say that intelligent design makes no testable predictions. And the theory does not provide a way to look for or investigate the designer. Instead, they maintain that intelligent design is an argument only because something has not yet been explained. As a result, evolutionists say that intelligent design supporters try to make the answer a supernatural one.

Finally, evolutionists argue that because these complex

organisms are not perfect, a designer can be ruled out. For example, the structures and genetic makeup of many organisms are inconsistent with the demands of design.

"In the 19th century people disagreed with the principle of evolution because it seemed to undermine their faith in God," says Dawkins. "Now there is a new way of trying to reinstate God, which is to say, well, we can see that evolution is true. Anybody ... can see that evolution is true. So we smuggle God back in by suggesting that he set up the conditions in which evolution might take place."[43]

The whole point of Darwinism is that it is self-sufficient, Dawkins says. The origin of the earth starts with essentially nothing, and by slow gradual degrees, it is built up from simple beginnings to complicated endings like humans, he explains.

"The beauty of that is that it works," he says. "Every stage is explained, every stage is understood. Nothing extra ... needs to be smuggled in."[44]

Science, Religion, or Philosophy?

Both supporters of Darwinism and supporters of intelligent design claim that their theories are rooted in science. But when arguing about the teaching of one or the other in public schools, supporters on both sides insist that religion and philosophy be kept out of the classroom.

In their arguments that "Darwinism is a philosophy" and "intelligent design is a religion," both sides point out how the other fails to meet the qualifications for science.

"Darwinism is a philosophy." Many advocates for intelligent design argue that Darwinism has become a faith itself. For example, Walter Bradley, the author of *The Mystery of Life's Origin* and a former professor at Texas A&M, says he feels people who believe that life emerged naturalistically need to have a great deal more faith than people who reasonably infer there is an intelligent designer.[45]

While many intelligent design supporters have no problem with some evolutionary processes, they do not believe that evolution accounts for everything. More specifically, they believe that some people now use Darwinism with the goal of making design unnecessary.

> The debate over the origins of life is one of the most fiercely argued points between intelligent design theorists and evolution theorists.

For example, evolutionists such as Richard Dawkins argue that Darwinism would have to be true even if there was no evidence for it. In other words, says Wells, what makes Dawkins so sure that Darwinism is true is not the evidence but the fact that it is the only materialistic explanation for the history of life.[46]

Joseph Naumann, the Roman Catholic archbishop of Kansas City, Kansas, says:

> It intrigues me that some proponents of evolution have been upset by what they perceive as injecting . . . theology into the science classroom, while they have appeared oblivious to the entwining of the philosophy of materialism with evolutionary theory for the past 150 years.[47]

Naumann says that evidence for natural selection should no longer be used as a springboard to teach the "grand assumptions" of materialism. He suggests letting the scientific facts speak for themselves without philosophical explanations.

"I'm convinced that sometime in the not-too-distant future . . . people will look back in amazement and say 'How could anyone have believed this?'" says Wells. "Darwinism is merely materialistic philosophy masquerading as science, and people are recognizing it for what it is."[48]

"Intelligent design is a religion." When evolutionists want to point out that intelligent design is not really science but instead a form of religion, they usually point to the court cases. The most recent case is the *Kitzmiller* case in Dover, Pennsylvania.

Following that trial, the judge's written opinion included a number of remarks about intelligent design theory. For example, he said that "the evidence at trial [shows] that ID is nothing less than the [descendant] of creationism. . . . No serious alternative to God as the designer has been proposed."[49]

Evolutionists also say that intelligent design does not have any significant scientific support. They argue that there has been very little written about it in respected scientific journals. And most scientists reject it as an alternate explanation for natural selection. The reason, they say, is simple: Intelligent design is just another form of creationism.

"The intelligent-design people are trying to mislead people into thinking that the reference to science as an ongoing critical inquiry permits them to teach ID crap in the schools," says David Thomas, president of New Mexicans for Science and Reason.[50]

Matzke says that teachers have to give kids the basics and the best information available from the scientific community.

"That means teaching the foundational central ideas in the field and not every wacky fringe idea that seems good to somebody," he adds. "It's not a matter of fairness. It's preparing people for college and the world economy—that's really what the game is."[51]

Other Arguments

There are a number of other arguments surrounding the evolution versus intelligent design debate. These include arguments such as "evolution is just a theory," arguments over the natural world versus the supernatural world, and others.

Evolution is just a theory. The "evolution is just a theory" argument is an old argument—and was primarily used by creationists. This exact wording, however, is not used very often by intelligent design supporters. Instead, what intelligent design supporters want to show is that evolution is not a proven fact.

Want to Know More?

The arguments surrounding evolution and intelligent design are extensive. As a result, only the primary arguments were presented in this chapter. If you would like to know more about the arguments surrounding evolution and intelligent design, here is a list of topics to research. You can use the list of organizations at the back of the book to begin your research, or research the terms listed below on the Internet:

- Cambrian explosion
- homology
- archaeopteryx
- peppered moths
- Darwin's finches

- mutant fruit flies
- second law of thermodynamics
- fossil horses
- Darwin's Tree of Life

And so, they say, it should not be promoted rigidly in school classrooms.

Although this is probably the same message creationists wanted to convey, intelligent design supporters feel that calling evolution "just a theory" does not communicate the true message. The message they want to communicate is that "particles-to-people evolution is an unsubstantiated *hypothesis* or *conjecture.*"[52]

On the other hand, evolutionists say that strictly speaking, calling the theory of evolution "only a theory" is true. What is wrong, they say, is the idea that this statement tries to convey. The term *theory*, when used in science, does not imply tentativeness or lack of certainty.

"In the real world, we must deal with levels of certainty based on observed evidence," says Mark Isaak. "The more and better evidence we have for something, the more certainty we assign to it. . . . What evolution has is what any good scientific claim has—evidence, and lots of it."[53]

The natural and the supernatural—do both belong in science? According to supporters of evolution, science is by definition a self-limited focus on the natural world. It cannot speak about the supernatural world.

Evolutionists believe that allowing supernatural explanations into the classroom goes against the very definition of science. And, they say, intelligent design theory is largely based on supernatural explanations.

"Science does not try to explain God or the supernatural," says Tim Berra, a professor at The Ohio State University in Mansfield. "Science's domain is the natural world and the scientific method has been spectacularly successful at discovering knowledge about this world."[54]

From the intelligent design perspective, distinctions between the natural and the supernatural are not important. They say the real issue is not between natural laws and miracles, but between undirected natural causes and intelligent ones.

"Whether an intelligent cause is located within or outside nature . . . is a separate question from whether an intelligent cause has operated," says William Dembski.[55]

He says the point is that even if something is miraculously created, it can still be studied. For example, the bacteria flagellum is still a bacteria flagellum whether it evolved or was created two seconds ago. It can still be taken apart and studied. Scientists can figure out how it works, examine its parts, and try making changes to it—regardless of how it came into existence.[56]

All in all, both sides of the evolution versus intelligent design debate are trying to appeal to the intelligence and the wisdom of the American people to resolve the dispute.

The Battleground: Evolution and Intelligent Design in Education

Many people say that public education in America is in crisis. But the reasons vary depending on whom you talk to. The worries run the gamut. Some wonder whether or not U.S. students are lagging behind other nations' students in science because of evolution debates. Others argue that students are being taught to blindly accept material and regurgitate facts in order to pass standardized tests when they should be encouraged to think for themselves and critically analyze material. And finally, some worry that public education is negatively impacting the moral fabric of our country because of the ideas and philosophies that are taught.

Because public schools are often considered the training ground for the next generation of leaders, it is not surprising then that the battle over evolution and intelligent design is fought so fiercely in our nation's public school districts. Both sides are worried about what the country's educational systems will produce.

The Evolving Game Plan

Those active in the century-old struggle against teaching evolution exclusively have used a number of tactics to advance their ideas. These methods include everything from "balanced treatment," which required evolution and creationism to be taught side by side, to textbook disclaimers, which were stickers that emphasized that evolution is just a theory.

Recently, the push for change in how evolution is taught has been at a state level. Statewide science standards have become the target for several reasons. First, influencing statewide curriculum standards has a broader impact than local school board decisions. In addition, advocates can avoid dealing with local activists who may not be fully informed. Also, the state decision makers are elected, which makes them responsive to political pressure.

State science standards have only been around since the late 1980s and early 1990s. They are the result of a national movement to bring more accountability to education. Some indicate that the political fight over state standards in education has actually strengthened the teaching of evolution. In 2000, ten states did not mention evolution in their curriculum standards. Today, only Florida, Kentucky, Mississippi, and Oklahoma omit evolution from their standards.

Overall, no other theory has attracted as much controversy, political involvement, and legal attention as evolution.

It's Not Just for School Anymore

The battle over evolution has expanded. It is moving beyond the classroom and into summer camp. In fact, a number of the country's summer camps around the country are taking on the battle—and science camps are not the only ones. According to the Christian Camp and Conference Association, 50 percent of its members have a science curriculum about God's creation. The association includes both summer camps and year-round after-school programs and reaches six million kids every year.[1]

For example, campers at Timber-lee Christian Center in Wisconsin can go on a seven-room "Creation Walk," showcasing the Bible's seven days of creation. The camp's outdoor education director says: "The curriculum is designed to open their eyes so when they go back to school (and hear about evolution) they say, 'Oh, that sounds goofy!'"[2]

For those who prefer camps that have a bent toward evolution, there are a number of options. For example, the Chalice Camp in California, sponsored by a Unitarian Universalist Church, teaches children about human origins through song, dance, and drama. And Camp Quest, an atheist camp located in several locations throughout the United States, teaches kids about evolution, separation of church and state, and other related topics. One of the camp's directors says: "Our sense is that evolution isn't being taught enough (in schools) or that people are becoming afraid to teach it."[3]

A Critical Test

There have been numerous battles over science standards both at the state and local levels. Perhaps the most notable battle is the Dover, Pennsylvania, case. This court case, known as *Kitzmiller* v. *Dover District Board of Education*, was the first federal court case that addressed teaching intelligent design in public schools.

In the fall of 2004, Dover school board members mandated that teachers read a statement about evolution to a ninth-grade biology class, saying that evolution is a theory and a theory is not a fact. It also pointed to "gaps in the theory" and indicated that intelligent design was another explanation. The statement also told students that if they wanted more information, the library had the textbook *Of Pandas and People*. Finally, the statement encouraged students to keep an open mind.

As a result of the decision, three school board members resigned in protest, and district science teachers refused to read the statement. By December 2004, the community's frustration had reached a peak, and there was a lawsuit in the works.

Tammy Kitzmiller, a mother of two teenagers, was the lead plaintiff in the case. She and ten other parents sued the district. They said that with the required statement, the board was imposing a religious view on students.

Kitzmiller and the other parents were represented by the ACLU and the Pepper Hamilton law firm. The Americans United for Separation of Church and State and the National Center for Science Education also backed them. Meanwhile, the school district was represented by the Thomas More Law Center, a nonprofit legal firm that fights for religious freedom in the United States.

A twist in the case was that the Discovery Institute, a leading supporter of intelligent design, opposed the board's action from the start. The institute is a national organization that advocates that science teachers take a broader approach to teaching the theory of evolution. It also supports the work of scientists and scholars who are researching challenges to the theory like intelligent design. As a result, they did not participate as a group in the trial.

Casey Luskin of the Discovery Institute says when school boards like Dover mandate the teaching of such a new and controversial idea, they politicize a debate that should take place among scientists.

"School boards are best advised to require the teaching of something many scientists already agree upon: that neo-Darwinism fails to account for much of what we observe in biology," Luskin says.[4]

The trial, which began in late September 2005, lasted forty days. It included expert testimony from several notable biologists, including Kenneth Miller, Robert Pennock, and Michael Behe. In December 2005, the federal judge hearing the case ruled in favor of Kitzmiller and the other plaintiffs.

"The citizens of the Dover area were poorly served by the members of the board who voted for the ID policy," U.S. District Judge John E. Jones III said in his 139-page opinion.[5]

In the end, the battle divided the community. Voters replaced the pro-intelligent design board members with new board members. The newly elected members pledged to undo the work of the previous board.

The Guiding Principles

Congress shall make no law respecting an establishment of religion, or prohibiting the free exercise thereof.
        —U.S. Constitution, Amendment I

These words are often used as the guiding principles when dealing with the evolution versus intelligent design debate. The Constitution is the basis for government in the United States. This document spells out how government is formed, who makes up the government, and how to pass and amend laws.

There are two clauses in the Constitution that guarantee freedom of religion. These clauses, which are found in the First Amendment, include the Establishment Clause and the Free Exercise Clause. Even though these clauses were meant to serve common values, there is a lot of tension between the two.

In general, the Establishment Clause prohibits the government from establishing a national religion or preferring one religion over another. It is sometimes referred to as the "separation of church and state." The Free Exercise Clause has often

The Implications of Judge Jones's Opinion

Supporters on both sides of the evolution versus intelligent design debate have reviewed Judge Jones's opinion and have drawn different conclusions. Law professor Stephen Gey says that the most striking aspects of the judge's opinion are the ways in which he addresses intelligent design—not his constitutional analysis. Gey points to three aspects of the written opinion as examples:

1. Judge Jones said the addition of intelligent design to the curriculum had a religious effect. He also said that if intelligent design is included in science classes, this would suggest that the government endorsed a particular religion.
2. Judge Jones's tone was harsh at times regarding the school board's attempts to advance intelligent design. At one point, he said the board's efforts were an "utter waste of (money) and personal resources."
3. Judge Jones said he felt intelligent design was not a true science and was not accepted by the scientific community.[6]

Intelligent design supporters see the decision in a slightly different light. Overall, they feel Jones drew conclusions and made statements beyond what he was qualified to do. Additionally, they feel these statements are not accurate. For example, Jones found that there was no difference between creationism and intelligent design. But according to supporters there is a very big difference. Both ID and creationism hold that there is a creator or designer; however, creationism holds that God created Earth and life on it is pretty much as it presently exists, while ID accepts that Earth and life are billions of years old and that life has evolved. It even accepts some degree of common ancestry among species.

"(Intelligent design) simply finds the claim that all life evolved from a single organism not to best fit the available evidence," says Robert Robb, a columnist. He adds that intelligent design supporters do not want to ban teaching evolution or require that it be taught. Robb says their focus is to see a more cautious presentation of the theory, including acknowledging its scientific evaluations.[7]

Robb says that Judge Jones "defined science and determined that the scientific claims of intelligent design were invalid, neither of which are exactly legal questions best decided by a single lawyer."[8]

Jones also ruled on the nature of theology as well, he says. He determined that evolution "in no way conflicts with, nor does it deny, the existence of a divine creator."[9]

"That's not necessarily so," Robb explains. "Much of evolutionary teaching contends that life on Earth is the accidental and unplanned result of exclusively natural processes. (It rules out) life on Earth being the willed outcome of a Creator."[10]

been interpreted to include two freedoms—the freedom to believe and the freedom to act.

Establishment Clause. When the country was founded, there were other countries in the world that had a national religion and supported that religion financially. Many believe the Establishment Clause was designed to keep that from happening in America. However, there are two different opinions on how far this clause should go in protecting people today.

People who see a broader meaning in the Establishment Clause point to writings by Thomas Jefferson and James Madison. Jefferson and Madison suggested that we needed "a wall of separation" between church and state. What they meant was that the government should not be combined with religion. Meanwhile, people who see a more narrow meaning in the Establishment Clause point out that this same group also opened their meetings with prayer. Jefferson, Madison, and others also voted to use federal dollars to establish Christian missions. The extent to which this clause is enforced is decided by the Supreme Court.[11]

The United States did not really have a legal interpretation of the Establishment Clause until 1947. At that time, the Court determined that some activity by the government related to religion was constitutional. In the case of *Everson* v. *Board of Education*, the judge found that it was constitutional to reimburse parochial students for bus transportation. He said that it was in the state's best interest to get kids safely to school.[12]

Decisions that followed showed that the "wall of separation" was a shifting barrier depending on the issue. For example, in 1948 the Supreme Court ruled that inviting religious leaders to public schools to teach optional religion classes was a violation of the Establishment Clause. However, in 1952, the Court upheld the decision to allow students "released time," excusing them from school so they could attend religious programs.[13]

Perhaps the most influential case in interpreting the

Establishment Clause was the 1962 case *Engel* v. *Vitale.* The Court ruled that New York's practice of beginning school days with prayer violated the Establishment Clause. As a result, numerous cases followed involving school prayer. In general, the Court has shown that they will likely strike down anything that is seen as a state endorsement of religion.

Free Exercise Clause. The Free Exercise Clause prohibits the government from interfering with a person's practice of their religion. However, the United States still monitors religious practices. Of particular interest are practices like human sacrifice, use of drugs, and other criminal acts. In these cases, the government tries to balance the freedom to practice religion with the safety and well-being of others.

In general, the courts demand that any laws restricting religious practices do so only to the extent necessary. The laws should demonstrate that restricting religious practices is in the state's best interest, such as protecting others from bodily harm.[14]

Let Freedom Ring

The United States is proud of its freedoms, especially the freedom of speech. It is probably one of the most fiercely protected rights in this country. For this reason, it is not surprising that under the umbrella of freedom of speech we often find two other freedoms—academic freedom and student rights. These two concepts are often brought into the debate over evolution versus intelligent design.

Academic freedom. Academic freedom is the freedom to pursue knowledge wherever it may lead without undue or unreasonable interference. Ideally, teachers have the right to conduct their classrooms and studies in a way that they believe is most consistent with the pursuit of truth.

Although academic freedom is not specifically mentioned in the Constitution, the Supreme Court has said it is a freedom

Students and a teacher in a science class. Issues of academic and religious freedom are involved in the debate over evolution.

that should be protected alongside the country's other freedoms. For example, in a 1967 court case, *Keyishian* v. *Board of Regents of the University of the State of New York*, the court said that academic freedom was entitled to the protection of the First Amendment.[15]

Student rights. For many years, students' rights—including the right to free speech, free press, free association, and the freedom from searches and seizures—have been debated. More recently, supporters of intelligent design have been arguing that many science classrooms are hostile toward Christian students' beliefs and are thus trampling on their freedom of religion.

"When the state's schools teach a student who believes in creation by God, that evolution is a fact, even though it cannot be proved to be a fact, the state is telling the student that his or her religious belief is falsehood," says Robert Kofahl, who holds a doctorate in chemistry and is the author of *The Creation Explanation.* As a result, Kofahl argues, the state is violating the religious student's free exercise rights.[16]

The whole area of student rights is a relatively new topic. With regard to day-to-day class work, the courts have said that there is a difference between exposing students to material they might find objectionable, which is all right, and attempting to coerce a student to develop a political or religious viewpoint, which is not. Parents who can prove that coercion is taking place will have a much better chance of winning in court.[17]

What's more, the Supreme Court said in the case of *Committee for Public Education* v. *Nyquist* that the First Amendment does not forbid all mention of religion in public schools. It is the advancement of religion that is prohibited. Some would argue that any religious topic is fair game in schools if presented objectively.[18]

Samuel Jefferson, a newspaper editor and historian in central Ohio who supports evolution, feels intelligent design is better suited for history class. He says in history classes you have a "marketplace of ideas."

"If a school proposed a class called the 'Evolution of Science' they could discuss ideas like Paley's watchmaker theory, Darwinism, creationism and intelligent design," he explains. "When you are coming at it from that approach, it is a whole different animal."[19]

Designing the Curriculum

Sheree Hied, a mother of five, was one of the parents in Dover, Pennsylvania, who was grateful when the school district offered students alternatives to evolution. Numerous polls indicate that she is not alone. The majority of Americans want to see intelligent design taught alongside evolution.

"I think we as Americans, regardless of our beliefs should be able to freely access information because people fought and died for our freedoms," Hied says.[20]

Josh Van Dop, who majored in biology at Hope College, a Christian college in Michigan, thinks that intelligent design is a counterpart to evolution. Even though he does not consider intelligent design "hard science," he says he feels it should be presented in biology class.

"I do not think natural selection goes all the way back to the origin of species. The natural selection theory is a slow-working theory. It takes many, many years for one characteristic to change to have the level of detail I have seen in organisms," he says.[21]

But the National Science Teachers Association (NSTA) says that administrators and teachers should not give in to pressure to downplay the significance of evolution or to include "nonscientific" ideas in biology classes. Instead, they offer the following suggestions regarding the teaching of evolution:

- Science classes should emphasize evolution's importance in understanding other areas of science.

- Science teachers should not advocate religious interpretations of nature and should not judge the personal beliefs of students.

- Policy makers and school administrators should not require the teaching of intelligent design (or other related subjects).

- Community involvement in developing science curriculum is an important part of our society and should be encouraged. But the professional responsibility to provide quality science education should not be compromised.

- Textbooks should emphasize evolution as a unifying concept. Publishers should not be required or volunteer to include disclaimers in textbooks.[22]

According to the NSTA, there is no longer a debate among scientists about *whether* evolution has taken place. However, there is considerable debate about *how* evolution has taken place. For example, scientists still disagree about the processes and mechanisms they say produce change. And they disagree about what has happened during the history of the universe.

"Evolution as with any aspect of . . . science is continually open to and subject to experimental and observational testing," the association says.[23]

Of Pandas and People

Of Pandas and People is a textbook originally published in 1989 by the Foundation of Thought and Ethics. A revised version was produced in 1993. According to the publisher, the textbook was meant only as a supplement to other biology textbooks and not a replacement. The goal, they say, was to help students understand origins and to show that information can be looked at in different ways. "We don't propose to give final answers," they add.[24]

The 1993 version included a Note to Teachers written by Mark Hartwig and Stephen Meyer of the Discovery Institute. In the note, they do not deny that *Of Pandas and People* is one-sided.

"*Pandas* makes no bones about being a text with a point of view," they say. "Because it was intended to be supplemental text, the authors saw no value in . . . rehashing the (more traditional) accounts given by (other) textbooks."[25]

In their Note to Teachers, they also encourage teachers to embrace controversy. They argue that controversy gives teachers the opportunity to engage their students at a deeper level.

"Instead of filling young minds with discrete facts and vocabulary lists, teachers can show their students the rough-and-tumble of genuine scientific debate," they say. "In this way, students begin to understand how science really works . . . (and they) learn something about the human dimension of science."[26]

But supporters of evolution are skeptical. For example, Kenneth Miller says when he opened the Pandas book he was disappointed.

"When I first opened the pages of *Pandas* . . . I expected a text that might genuinely challenge students to examine the assumptions of what they had learned and evaluate scientific theory in an objective manner," Miller says. "What I found instead was a document that contrived not to teach, but to mislead."[27]

Miller also points out that the book is riddled with inaccuracies and calls the book "a collection of half-truths, distortions, and outright falsehoods that attempts to misrepresent biology and mislead students. . . ."[28]

"There is a great deal that we do not know about the origin of life on this planet," he says, "but that does not mean that science is obliged to pretend that it knows *nothing*. . . ."[29]

What's more, Nick Matzke of the National Center for Science Education says that the *Pandas* textbook came first—before the research to support it.

"If ID ever does succeed, it will be the first movement in the history of science that *began* in a high school textbook and *then* 'filtered up' to acceptance by the scientific research community," he says.[30]

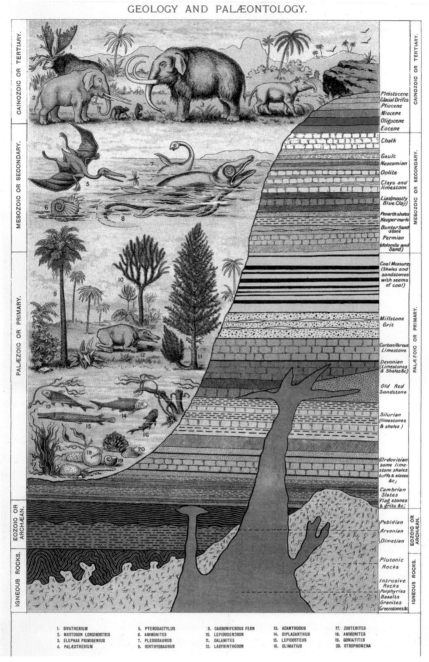

GEOLOGY AND PALÆONTOLOGY.

1.	SIVATHERIUM	5.	PTERODACTYLUS	9.	CARBONIFEROUS FERN	13.	ACANTHODUS	17.	ZOSTERITES
2.	MASTODON LONGIROSTRIS	6.	AMMONITES	10.	LEPIDODENDRON	14.	DIPLACANTHUS	18.	AMMONITES
3.	ELEPHAS PRIMIGENIUS	7.	PLESIOSAURUS	11.	CALAMITES	15.	LEPIDOSTEUS	19.	GONIATITES
4.	PALÆOTHERIUM	8.	ICHTHYOSAURUS	12.	LABYRINTHODON	16.	CLIMATIUS	20.	STROPHOMENA

A vintage illustration showing geological eras. While most scientists agree that evolution has taken place, there is still debate over how it occurred and the specific events that cause change.

Supporters of intelligent design say that while they still want evolution taught in schools, they want the approach to change. For example, Kofahl says there are a number of problems with the way in which evolution is being taught in schools today. Here are the problems he sees:

- Evolution is taught dogmatically. Kofahl says there is no place for dogma in science. What cannot be demonstrated as fact should not be taught as fact.

- Evolution is taught without criticism of weaknesses and failures. Kofahl says theories should not be protected. They should always be open to critical evaluation.

Survey Says U.S. Biology Books Score an "Unsatisfactory"

In a study conducted by the American Association for the Advancement of Science (AAAS) in 2000, all of the nation's top ten high school biology textbooks received an unsatisfactory rating.

"We couldn't recommend any of the available school textbooks," says Andrew Ahlgren, an associate director at AAAS.[31]

The review looked at how the biology books explained four different aspects of biology. These included (1) natural selection and evolution, (2) cell structure and function, (3) molecular basis of heredity, and (4) matter and energy transformation. Kenneth Miller's book *Biology*, one of the nation's more popular textbooks, was among those reviewed.

The report said that the books did not encourage students to examine their ideas or relate lessons to hands-on experiments and everyday life. Although some books scored well in specific categories, none were good at correcting misconceptions. Other problems included covering too many subjects, including easy-to-test trivia, and glossing over important concepts.

In response to the report, book publishers said that state science standards drive the content of the books. These standards are developed by teachers and local school administrators who consult with experts. So if scientists want to see better content, book publishers say scientists should get their message to the states. Ahlgren disagrees.

"They are saying teachers want this trash so we gave it to them," says Ahlgren.

". . . The teachers have never seen a good textbook."[32]

- Evolution is taught exclusively without competition—as the only scientifically acceptable way of thinking about the world. Kofahl says all ideas in science should be open to competition with alternative ideas.

- Evolution is taught under a flawed definition of science that is distorted by materialistic beliefs. Kofahl says that science is the method of studying natural order, not a belief system about it.[33]

"We do not want to attack anybody else's religious faith in the science classroom, but we want an end to the use of science and science instruction falsely as a weapon against God...." says Kofahl.[34]

Overall, Kofahl believes today's teaching of evolution is poor science and that stifling criticism and competition of ideas is poor teaching. And, he says protected and exclusive teaching of evolution denies student rights.[35]

The battle over education today is a lot like the Scopes trial of 1925, says Luskin. "Only now, the roles are reversed.... It is the Darwinists who seek to ban legitimate science from the classroom," he says. "May scientific truth and academic freedom ring."[36]

The Players: The Political Aspects of the Debate

In August 2005, when President George W. Bush said that both sides of the evolution versus intelligent design controversy should be taught in public schools, he added fuel to the fire of an already heated political debate.

"Part of education is to expose people to different schools of thought," President Bush said. "You're asking me whether or not people ought to be exposed to different ideas and the answer is yes." He also said that curriculum decisions should be made by local school districts rather than the federal government.[1]

His comments, which were made in a group interview

conducted by Texas reporters, brought about fierce criticism from evolution supporters. They argue that there is no educational basis for teaching intelligent design. Supporters also accuse intelligent design supporters of using political channels to advance their ideas when they should be building support for the theory in the scientific community. They say the evolution versus intelligent design debate is becoming a political battle that "threatens to weaken science teaching in a nation whose students already are lagging."[2]

John West, an associate director of the Discovery Institute, says the institute does not support teaching intelligent design in classrooms because the theory is so new. Instead, the institute supports an approach known as "teach the controversy," which promotes teaching "all the evidence relating to evolutionary theory," West explains.[3]

> When President George W. Bush said that both sides of the evolution vs. ID controversy should be taught in public schools, he added fuel to the fire of an already heated political debate.

"If high school or college students are capable of understanding evidence for evolution," he says, "certainly they could understand scientific criticisms of key parts of the theory, particularly the limit to the creative power of selection and random mutation."[4]

Samuel Jefferson says that "teach the controversy" is both a religious view and a political agenda. He believes schools would be better off staying away from political issues.

"There might be some people who say that evolution is a political agenda, but it is hard to beat fossil records. There is nothing political about a bone," he says. "There are other outlets for people who want to teach intelligent design. They can hold public seminars. There are a number of ways to get the information out."[5]

Eugenie Scott, director of the NCSE, says the problem with "teach the controversy" is that there is no controversy.

According to Scott, the disagreements in the scientific community have more to do with the pattern and process of evolution. She says you "will not find arguments over whether living things have common ancestors."[6]

Intelligent Design as a Movement

As a movement, the primary goal of ID supporters is to challenge the Darwinian approach to evolution, which implies that nature is all that is needed. Additionally, they want to change the way evolution, specifically Darwinism, is being taught in classrooms. They feel if teachers want to mention some of the research or ideas associated with intelligent design, they should have the academic freedom to do so.

To the dismay of some creationists, while intelligent design is compatible with some creationist beliefs, many supporters of the movement are unwilling to align themselves with biblical creationism.[7]

What's more, West is concerned that some groups may not fully understand intelligent design. "There is a concern that intelligent design has been hijacked by people who don't really know what it says," he explains. "We don't think it should be a political football."[8]

Although it is relatively new as a movement, intelligent design has quickly gained the support of legislators and textbook publishers. At a grassroots level, it is also attracting attention and sometimes support from teachers, parents, administrators, and school board members. This task is being accomplished through a number of strategies, including the "teach the controversy" campaign, "the wedge" strategy, and legislative attempts like the Santorum Amendment.

"Teach the controversy." The intelligent design movement's approach to challenging evolution in the classroom is often referred to as "teach the controversy." This political action campaign calls for schools to equip students with the ability to

analyze evolutionary theory critically. Additionally, supporters of intelligent design want the evidence both for and against evolution presented in the classroom. But they are being met with much opposition.

"Some [people] want to protect Darwinism," argues Jonathan Witt, an intelligent design supporter and coauthor of *Traipsing Into Evolution: Intelligent Design and the Kitzmiller v. Dover Decision*. "My hope is that these efforts will merely lead students to ask, 'What's the evidence they do not want us to see?'"[9]

Overall, the "teach the controversy" campaign appeals to the country's ideals of free speech, balance, and diversity. So it is not surprising that when Americans are polled, the majority favor teaching both the evidence for and the evidence against evolution. Additionally, advocates argue that teaching scientific controversies will engage students' interest and encourage them to think about how best to interpret the evidence.

Supporters even have convinced some evolutionists that teaching about the controversies is a good idea. For example, Michael Balter, a writer who has covered human evolution for *Science* magazine, says while he knows most scientists do not want a debate, he would like to see "'intelligent design' and science rumble."[10]

"The best way to teach the theory of evolution is to teach this contentious history," Balter says. "The most effective way to convince students that the theory is correct is to confront, not avoid, continuing challenges to it."[11]

"Let's encourage teachers to stage debates in their classrooms or in assemblies. Students can be assigned to one or the other side, and guest speakers can be invited," Balter suggests. "Among other things, students would learn that science, when properly done, reaches conclusions via experimentation, evidence and argument, not through majority view."[12]

Finally, Balter says that the monopoly that evolution has in

Students in a science lab. Supporters and opponents of intelligent design differ over whether it is "pseudoscience" or an area that should be covered in school.

classrooms only strengthens the movement's claims that scientists do not want to be challenged. More important, he says, it shields Darwinian theory from challenges that, when properly refuted, might win people over to evolutionary views.[13]

Overall, "teach the controversy" has been successful in getting states to try to take a more critical approach to teaching evolution in science classrooms. For example, five states—South Carolina, Minnesota, Pennsylvania, Kansas, and New Mexico—have approved statewide science standards that require a critical analysis of evolution. Additionally, none of these states require the teaching of intelligent design or other theories of origin. They simply require that the strengths and weaknesses of evolutionary theory be taught to students.[14]

"This means that in [the other forty-five states] Darwinian evolution is taught as sheer dogma," says Pete Chadwell, a ID supporter. "Scientific weaknesses are withheld from our students and Darwinian evolution is presented as a theory of origins that is [unquestionable]."[15]

Meyer says the ultimate question is whether states will agree that students should learn both sides of the controversy. Or, he asks, will "a 19th century theory ... be taught dogmatically to 21st century students?"[16]

The Wedge. The Wedge—or as it is more formally called, The Wedge of Truth—was developed by Phillip Johnson. The Wedge is a strategy used by religious scholars to cast doubt on the philosophical aspects of Darwinism.

The strategy's name comes from a method used for splitting logs. A log is something very solid and difficult to split. But by using a wedge, a log can eventually be split. The wedge penetrates a crack in the log and gradually widens the split.

Within the Wedge strategy, scientific materialism (sometimes called naturalism), appears to be a solid log. The widening crack is the difference between the facts revealed by science and the materialist (or naturalistic) philosophy that is found in scientific culture. The wedge represents the truth.

The details of the Wedge strategy are outlined in several of Johnson's books, including *Defeating Darwinism by Opening Minds, Darwin on Trial,* and *The Wedge of Truth: Splitting the Foundations of Naturalism.*

Overall, Johnson says he had two goals in developing the Wedge strategy. First, he wanted to make it possible to question naturalistic assumptions. Second, he wanted to redefine what is at issue in the creation-evolution controversy so that Christians and other believers in God could find common ground.[17]

"Protestants will disagree on various issues among themselves, Catholics will disagree with Protestants, and observant Jews will disagree with Christians," explains Johnson in his book *Defeating Darwinism by Opening Minds.* "What all these should agree on is that God—not some purposeless material process—is our true Creator....We should unite our energies to affirm the reality of God." Johnson says that Michael Behe's book, which describes irreducible complexity, represents the first broadening of the crack in the materialism "log."[18]

Johnson says the "enemies" of the Wedge are those who focus on side issues, such as the motivations of the Darwin doubters rather than encouraging a discussion of scientific evidence. "[They also] insist that the ruling scientific organizations be obeyed without question...."[19]

The Santorum Amendment. In June 2001, Rick Santorum, a Republican senator from Pennsylvania, proposed the Santorum Amendment. (An amendment is a change or revision to something that already exists.) This amendment, which addressed teaching evolution, was made to the Elementary and Secondary Education Act Authorization bill that was under consideration at the time. The proposed amendment passed the Senate with a vote of 91–8. The version of the bill that passed in the House of Representatives did not have a similar version of the

Santorum Amendment. So the House-Senate Conference Committee needed to reconsider the amendment and bring together the two versions of the bill. Ultimately, the Santorum Amendment was dropped from the bill in December 2001 and added to a conference report.

The compromise bill then was submitted to Congress and it passed. The bill, which was renamed the No Child Left Behind Act, was later signed into law by President Bush in 2002.

Although the Santorum Amendment (now called the "Santorum language") is not a legal mandate or part of No Child Left Behind Act, it is part of a conference report that is included with the law. The Santorum language is a revised version of the original amendment and says:

> The Conferees recognize that a quality science education should prepare students to distinguish the data and testable theories of science from religious and philosophical claims that are made in the name of science. Where topics are taught that may generate controversy (such as biological evolution), the curriculum should help students to understand the full range of scientific views that exist, why such topics may generate controversy, and how scientific discoveries can profoundly affect society.[20]

According to several senators and representatives, the Santorum Amendment was always intended as guidance, not a mandate. So it was appropriate to include it as report language.

"Report language provides official guidance from Congress on how statutory language should be enforced by other government agencies, and the Santorum language should be understood in this light," according to Representative John Boehner, Senator Judd Gregg, and Senator Rick Santorum in a letter to the Discovery Institute. "It is just as authoritative as other provisions in the report language of the Act, such as Congress's directive that 'mentoring services . . . not be limited to beginning teachers.'"[21]

"The Santorum language clarifies that public school

students are entitled to learn that there are differing scientific views on issues such as biological evolution," the congressmen explained. "...It is important that the implementation of [state] science standards not be used to censor debate on controversial issues in science."[22]

According to a report produced by the NCSE, the Santorum language is an "expression of the views of a few members of the House and Senate about the law."[23]

The report continues:

> Congress did not support the Santorum Amendment, as evidenced by the fact that it took it out of the final legislation. This suggests that the watered-down version that appeared [in the report] . . . was added at the [request] of a special interest group and did not receive the endorsement of Congress as a whole. In such situations, courts give legislative history little weight. . . . They in no way treat it as . . . 'federal law' on the subject.[24]

Results of Political Involvement

Many people feel the steady stream of proposed legislation and legal actions highlights the continuing frustration of American citizens with Darwinism's monopoly in science classrooms. As a result of this unrest, a number of policy makers are examining the controversy.

Most of the political battles surrounding the debate over evolution and intelligent design take place on state and local levels—namely on local school boards and state school boards. Of particular interest to those involved in the battle is the ongoing fight in Kansas.

In 2005, the Kansas State Board of Education passed state science standards encouraging students to seek "more adequate explanations of natural phenomena." While the curriculum standards do not mention intelligent design, many argue that intelligent design supporters lobbied for the changes.[25]

THE
LONDON SKETCH BOOK.

PROF. DARWIN.

This is the ape of form.
Love's Labor Lost, act 5, scene 2.

Some four or five descents since.
All's Well that Ends Well, act 3, sc. 7.

A cartoon from a London magazine in 1874 lampoons Darwin's theory of evolution. Even today, some people oppose teaching the theory.

A poll conducted by six news organizations in 2005 suggested that the state is divided on the issue. Half of Kansas thought evolution should be taught alongside intelligent design.[26]

Conservative Republicans, who are responsible for the current standards regarding evolution, have had control of the school board off and on since 1998. As a result, the standards have changed back and forth a great deal.

In 1999 and in 2005, the standards were set by conservatives and favored teaching the pros and cons of evolution. In 2001, when conservatives no longer held the majority of seats on the board, the standards set were more evolution friendly. Supporters of the latest standards argue that they merely encourage open discussion.

"Students need to have an accurate assessment of the state of the facts in regard to Darwin's theory," West says.[27]

The results from a recent election suggest that Kansas may change its state science standards yet again. Conservatives lost control of the school board in an August 2006 election.

At least two other states have been the site of battles over evolution and intelligent design: Ohio and California.

Ohio. Debates over evolution began in Ohio in 2000. At that time, the state's board of education began developing statewide academic standards. These standards provided an outline for standardized tests. But they did not impose any curriculum in the state's 613 local districts. A proposal to teach intelligent design alongside evolution was rejected.

In 2002, the board adopted standards requiring that tenth graders be able to "describe how scientists continue to investigate and critically analyze aspects of evolutionary theory." There also was a note that "this benchmark does not mandate the teaching or testing of intelligent design."[28]

This decision made Ohio one of the first states to single out evolution for "critical analysis" under the academic standards it adopted. The Discovery Institute had said that Ohio's critical analysis approach was a model for the nation. However, in February 2006, the board stripped the language from the curriculum.

Some speculate that the board feared a lawsuit, especially following the court ruling in Dover, Pennsylvania, in December 2005. The state's governor also had called for a legal review of the plan. And a national group of evolution defenders bombarded five board members with thirty thousand e-mail messages the week before the vote. These five people were considered crucial to the vote.[29]

"This just shows the extremism on the other side," West says. "They think Dover is their wedge to . . . stop . . . voluntary critical analysis of Darwin's theory in the classroom. They obviously don't think they can win in the court of public opinion on the issue, and that's why they're using scare tactics."[30]

California. In 2006, a group of parents sued a rural school district in California in federal court. They were opposed to an optional philosophy course called "Philosophy of Design," which promoted the idea of intelligent design. The parents said that the course, which was taught by a local minister's wife, was unconstitutional because of separation of church and state.

The Discovery Institute encouraged school district officials to settle. The district agreed to cancel the course and not offer another like it ever again.

"This sends a strong signal to school districts across the country that they cannot promote creationism or intelligent design as an alternative to evolution whether they do so in a science class or a humanities class," says Ayesha Khan, legal director for Americans United for Separation of Church and State.[31]

"[The course] was misconceived," says West. "It was almost

all about Biblical creationism, not intelligent design, and it also seemed lopsided."[32]

Battles over evolution and intelligent design are cropping up in states all across the nation. But it's not an easy matter to address. Wayne Carley, executive director of the National Association of Biology Teachers, says a large number of intelligent design supporters approach this issue as one of faith.

"We can argue that it's bad science, but people don't want to hear that," Carley says. "They are coming from a more basic gut level."[33]

The End Game: What the Future Holds

Darwinism has always been a tough sell to Americans. In fact, just fifteen years after Charles Darwin published his book in England, Charles Hodge, a Princeton theologian, responded with his own book—*What Is Darwinism?* In it, he argued that Darwin's denial of design in nature "is virtually the denial of God."

Hodge noted that Darwin might personally believe in a creator who had "called matter and a living germ into existence." But, he said, Darwinism implies that God then abandoned the universe to itself without any purpose, intervention, or guidance from him. Such a God, in Hodge's opinion, is then reduced to nonexistence—making Darwinism basically an atheistic viewpoint.[1]

It's been almost a century and a half since Hodge made those accusations. Yet Americans are still struggling with the idea of natural selection. While the battle may have changed somewhat over the years, it is still one that is hotly debated. And it looks like it is one that is far from over.

In fact, Edward Larson, an expert on the historical and legal issues surrounding teaching evolution, says the controversies will continue well into the future. Larson, who is also a law professor and Pulitzer Prize winner, says that the issue continues to resurface because "religion still matters greatly in America."[2]

According to some experts, part of the problem is that many people today believe, like Hodge, that evolution equates to atheism. Theistic scientists (those who believe that God used evolution to create the world) blame scientists like Richard Dawkins, the Oxford University zoologist and author of *The Blind Watchmaker* and *The God Delusion.*

Dawkins has called religion "the big lie." Additionally, he has said that the universe has no design, no purpose, no evil and no good—"nothing but blind, pitiless indifference." In the United States, where the majority of Americans believe in God, such ideas surely will cause problems.[3]

"The problem is perhaps less with believers who read the Bible as a literal account of creation, and more with believers who read Richard Dawkins as a literal account of evolution," says William Grassie, executive director of the Metanexus Institute, an organization devoted to reconciling religion and science.[4]

Scholars like Larson say the future direction of the debate could depend on the outcome of a case in Georgia, *Selman* v. *Cobb County School District.* In January 2005, a federal district judge said that the school district's required textbook stickers stating "evolution is a theory" violated the Establishment Clause.[5]

Currently, the case is before the eleventh U.S. Circuit Court of Appeals. Larson says that this case is worth watching, along with the Kansas teaching standards. These examples show that the controversy is not likely to die down soon.

"The controversy has tapped into a cultural divide," he says. "If history is any guide, then we're in for heavy weather again."[6]

The American Phenomenon

In other countries around the world, there is not much debate about evolution. In fact, Jon D. Miller of Northwestern University says, "we are out on a limb by ourselves." The distrust of evolution is almost entirely an American phenomenon.[7]

In fact, polls in thirty-four countries show the United States at the bottom when it comes to the acceptance of evolution. Only Turkey, which has a large sect of Muslim creationists, shows lower acceptance rates. Eighty-four percent or more of adults in Iceland, Denmark, Sweden, and France accept evolution. Meanwhile, 70 percent or more accept evolution in Japan, Britain, Norway, Belgium, Spain, and Germany.[8]

Although there is a high amount of support for science and technology among Americans, some still have concerns about the change science brings and about its conflicts with traditional religious beliefs. Fifty percent of Americans say that "we depend too much on science and not enough on faith."[9]

However, some psychology experts say that religious beliefs are only half the picture when it comes to doubts about Darwinism. They suggest that the public embraces intelligent design also because it is compatible with human intuition.

Psychologists suggest that intelligent design theorists have capitalized on the general public's skepticism. They say what stands in the way of evolutionary theory is not religion but the general public's belief that "common sense is a reliable guide to evaluating the natural world." With this in mind, it comes as no surprise that at least forty states are considering some type of action regarding evolution.[10]

How Might the Debate Evolve?

The federal court system indicated where it stands on intelligent design in the *Kitzmiller* case. However, efforts to advance the theory have in no way stalled. Scholars predict that future proposals are less likely than earlier ones to even mention the words "intelligent design."

For example, a proposal being considered in Missouri would require science teachers in grades six through twelve to "support the truthful identity of scientific information." Additionally, evolution gets special attention: "If a theory or hypothesis of biological origins is taught, a critical analysis ... shall be taught."[11]

Likewise, in Indiana, proposed legislation would keep the state board of education from adopting a textbook that "contains information, descriptions, conclusions, or pictures that are false." This type of proposal moves the debate from the school board to textbook committees. These committees often consist of scientists, teachers, parents, and other concerned citizens. As a result, scholars believe that arguments about scientific facts and theories could rage endlessly.

Erica Van Dop, a central Ohio resident and premed major, says that the intelligent design movement should coin a term to help better describe its ideas:

> In scientific medical literature they document everything that has happened and then they say "this would be an unscientific finding." [Intelligent design scientists should do the same.] They should coin a term like "miracle" or say that this is "unexplainable by natural law, but this has occurred." [This type of information] is documented in other journals. They should not try to force intelligent design under the guise of straight, natural science.[12]

Richard Dawkins, author of *The God Delusion*, holds that science proves that God does not exist. Supporters of evolution who do believe in God blame Dawkins, among others, for causing people to equate evolution with atheism.

Finally, evolution experts like Eugenie Scott of the National Center for Science Education predicts that a new "strain" of intelligent design will emerge in the years to come. Scott says she expects to see a new name for the movement—something like "sudden emergence theory" or "creative evolution."[13]

Intelligent design implies a designer, she says. Once you have an agent who is capable of miraculous things like the creation of a bacterial flagellum, then you are talking about God. She predicts intelligent design supporters will come up with an "agentless form" to promote their ideas.[14]

Psychology experts agree. They say scientists need to make drastic changes in how science is taught so that students are able to understand the scientific method and interpret the world accurately. It is only a matter of time before an even stronger version of intelligent design emerges, and students need to be ready to evaluate it.[15]

Can Science and Religion Be Reconciled?

Science without religion is lame; religion without science is blind.
—Albert Einstein

Like many other great scientists, Albert Einstein was convinced that there was an intelligent life behind the universe. In fact, some surveys indicate that scientists today may be just as likely to believe in God as other people.

For example, a 1997 survey in *Nature* found 40 percent of scientists believe in a God to whom one can pray and expect an answer. Interestingly, that is the same percentage of scientists who were believers when the survey was taken eighty years earlier. And many see no conflict between their faith and their work.[16]

But it is not really science as a whole that needs to be reconciled with religion but instead a very small aspect of science—Darwinism. Some scientists today use Darwin's theory under the assumption that it is a complete explanation of our existence and that God is not needed. This idea conflicts with the idea that we are created in the image of God, which is a central part of Christianity, Judaism, and Islam. For this reason, it is difficult for the two ideas to coexist.

> In other countries, there is not much debate about evolution. In fact, Jon D. Miller of Northwestern University says, "we are out on a limb by ourselves."

"[Darwinism] is controversial for the same reason that you can start a fight by . . . saying something about somebody's mother," explains Kenneth Miller. "It concerns where we're from, what our status is as human beings, and how we relate to the rest of life on Earth. That will always make it a controversial idea."[17]

According to Brian Greene, a physicist and author of *The Fabric of Cosmos*, science and religion operate in different realms. Scientists can never rule out religion, he says.

"Science is very good at answering the 'how' questions," Greene says. ". . . But it is woefully inadequate in addressing the 'why' questions."[18]

In fact, some argue that scientific discoveries may even draw scientists closer to God. "Even as science progresses . . . there will still remain a 'why' at the end," according to Ted Sargent, a nanotechnology expert at the University of Toronto. ". . . This is where many people will find God."[19]

Others believe that as long as some use Darwinism to insist that there is no need for God, then the two world views will never be compatible.

"Darwinists think that naturalism is the only answer, but ninety percent of the American people disagree with them," says Jonathan Wells. "It's time for the philosophical naturalists . . . to engage in some serious discussion with their fellow citizens."[20]

Will "Teach the Controversy" Prevail?

Nearly twenty years ago, literature professor Gerald Graff coined the phrase "teach the controversy." Graff was encouraging teachers to present students with conflicting arguments relevant to the times—for instance, presenting classes with extreme opinions about such books as *Moby Dick*—and using the debate to engage students. He elaborated on his ideas in the book, *Beyond the Culture Wars: How Teaching the Conflicts Can Revitalize American Education.*

Graff says when intelligent design supporters began using the slogan, he felt like his pocket had been picked. He also felt like religious conservatives were using his ideas to impose their ideas on schools. Feelings aside, though, Graff says that a case can be made for teaching the controversy between Darwinism and intelligent design.

Although Graff does not feel that both sides are equal, he does feel a debate would help clarify the issue. A debate also would encourage both students and teachers to think. At times, the truth and validity of an idea should not be the only factors considered when deciding what material to present to students, he says. Even false ideas can be extremely useful in developing problem-solving skills and can add value to the curriculum, he says.

"If the goal of education is to get students to think, then just telling students their doubts about Darwin are wrong is not going to be effective," says Graff. "And teachers being forced to engage their religious critics and explain why they believe in evolution might be a healthy thing for those teachers."[21]

What's more, Graff says that a classroom debate between intelligent design and evolution might be just the thing to wake up students who sleep during science. The result might be

More than one hundred years ago, the discovery of prehistoric fossils, such as those of dinosaurs, caused tension between science and religion. Today, that tension seems to be increasing as more discoveries are made.

students who have a clear understanding of science. In any case, Graff says teachers may have to teach the controversy anyway.

"If many American students now bring faith-based skepticism about evolution with them into classrooms . . . then there's a sense in which the controversy has already penetrated the classroom," he says. "Schools and colleges may not be teaching the controversy between faith and science, but it's there in the classroom anyway. . . . Teachers can act as if their students' doubts about evolution don't exist, but pretending that your students share your beliefs when you know they don't is a notorious prescription for bad teaching."[22]

Charles Haynes, a senior scholar with the First Amendment Center, cautions that "teach the controversy" could be a recipe for confusion and conflict. He says real curriculum reform and more teacher education are needed first.

"If school boards are serious about fostering 'critical thinking' and 'promoting tolerance and acceptance of a diversity of opinions,'" Haynes says, "then they must prepare teachers to teach about the debate in ways that are accurate, fair, informed—and grounded in good science."[23]

What this means is providing the resources so teachers can get it right. They need to have the latest evidence and be well informed about both sides, he says.

"Teachers can (and should) let kids in on the controversy—that's what education is all about—but only if they fully understand what the controversy is all about," he says. "It would also help if science teachers were clear about the limits of science. . . . Science education must avoid making metaphysical or religious claims in the guise of science."[24]

He uses the example of Carl Sagan, a popular American scientist, to illustrate his point. When Sagan said that "the universe is all there was, all there is, and all there ever will be," he was making a faith statement—not a scientific observation, Haynes explains.[25]

Moreover, Haynes believes that the already crowded science curriculum cannot accommodate the big questions like the relationship between religion and science. Other big questions include the implications of science for morality and ethical dilemmas posed by modern technology. He says for students to consider all those questions, the country needs courses in philosophy, ethics, and religion. But these courses are rarely offered, even as electives.

"There are no winners in this battle," Haynes concludes. "But there are losers. By failing to agree on how to teach fairly and critically the philosophical, moral, scientific and religious issues that confront our society, we fail our students. They lose. We all lose."[26]

Chapter Notes

Chapter 1 The Rivals: An Overview of the Controversy

1. Author's interview with [name withheld], July 2006.

2. Author's interview with Erica and Josh Van Dop, August 2006.

3. "The Evolution-Creationism Controversy: A Chronology," *Famous Trials in American History—Tennessee v. John Scopes "The Monkey Trial" 1925*, n.d., <http://www.law.umkc.edu/faculty/projects/ftrials/scopes/scopeschrono.html> (December 27, 1007).

4. Raju Cheblum, "75 Years After the Scopes Trial Pitted Science Against Religion, the Debate Goes On," *CNN.com*, July 13, 2000, <http://archives.cnn.com/2000/LAW/07/13/scopes.monkey.trial> (April 22, 2006).

5. "The Evolution-Creationism Controversy: A Chronology."

6. Cheblum.

7. "Day 7: Darrow Examines Bryan," *Famous Trials in American History—Tennessee v. John Scopes "The Monkey Trial" 1925*, n.d., <http://www.law.umkc.edu/faculty/projects/ftrials/scopes/scopes2.htm> (February 1, 2008).

8. Ibid.

9. Ibid.

10. Cheblum.

11. Ibid.

12. Ibid.

13. Ibid.

14. Austin Cline, "The Scopes Monkey Trial: The Aftermath," *About.com*, <http://atheism.about.com/library/FAQs/evo/blevo_law_scopes_after.htm> (July 22, 2006).

15. Ibid.

16. "The Monkey Trial: A closer look at Hollywood's *Inherit the Wind*," n.d., <http://www.themonkeytrial.com> (July 23, 2006).

17. Cline.

18. "Poll: Creationism Trumps Evolution," *CBS News*, November 22, 2004, <http://www.cbsnews.com/stories/2004/11/22/opinion/polls/printable657083.shtml> (April 22, 2006).

19. "Poll: Creationism Trumps Evolution."

20. Ibid.

21. "Public Divided on Origins of Life," The Pew Forum, August 30, 2005, <http://pewforum.org/surveys/origin> (April 22, 2006).

22. "Can a Theory Evolve Into a Law?" A Moment of Science Library, 2003, <http://amos.indiana.edu/library/scripts/theory.html> (June 10, 2006).

23. "Public Divided on Origins of Life."

24. "For Almost All Americans, There Is God," *CBS News*, April 13, 2006, <http://www.cbsnews.com/stories/2006/04/13/opinion/polls/printable1498219.shtm> (April 22, 2006).

Chapter 2 The Defender: A Closer Look at Evolution

1. "NABT's Statement on Teaching Evolution," National Association of Biology Teachers, 2004, <http://www.nabt.org/sites/S1/index.php?p=65> (July 20, 2005).

2. "Understanding Evolution," University of California Museum of Paleontology and the National Center for Science Education, 2006, <http://evolution.berkeley.edu/evolibrary/article/0_0_0/evo_18> (August 28, 2006).

3. Ibid.

4. Ibid.

5. Warren D. Allmon, "Evolution and Creationism: A Guide for Museum Docents," Museum of the Earth, Ithaca, NY, August 18, 2005, p. 6

6. Cath Senker, *Charles Darwin* (Austin, Texas: Steck-Vaughn, 2002), p. 27.

7. David Quammen, "Was Darwin Wrong?" *National Geographic Magazine*, <http://magma.nationalgeographic.com/ngm/0411/feature1/fulltext.html> (February 1, 2008).

8. "Naturalistic Origin of Species," Veritas Forum at Rice University, n.d., <http://www.ruf.rice.edu/~veritas/truth.htm> (February 4, 2008).

9. "Evolution: Misconceptions of Modern Evolutionary Biology," *Wikipedia*, n.d., <http://en.wikipedia.org/wiki/Evolution> (February 4, 2008).

10. Phillip E. Johnson, *Defeating Darwinism by Opening Minds* (Downers Grove, Ill.: InterVarsity Press, 1997), pp. 15–16.

11. Lee Strobel, *The Case for a Creator* (Grand Rapids, Mich.: Zondervan, 2004), pp. 31–32.

12. Ibid., p. 32.

13. Ibid.

14. "Hanken, Pace Give Lesson to Behe, Wells," Press Release, National Center for Science Education—Setting the Record Straight, September 17, 2001, <http://www.ncseweb.org/article.asp?category=12> (February 1, 2008).

Chapter 3 The Challenger: A Closer Look at Intelligent Design

1. John Roach, "Does Intelligent Design Threaten the Definition of Science?" *National Geographic News*, April 27, 2005, <http://news.nationalgeographic.com/news/2005/04/0427_050427_intelligent_design.html> (August 29, 2006).

2. Ibid.

3. Tristan Abby, "The Myths Surrounding Intelligent Design," *The Stanford Daily*, February 21, 2006, Discovery Institute News, <http://www.discovery.org/scripts/viewDB/index.php?command=view&id=3275> (April 14, 2006).

4. "What Is Intelligent Design?" *Access Research Network*, n.d., <http://www.arn.org/idfaq/what%20is%20intelligent%20design.htm> (August 28, 2006).

5. Daniel Engber, "Creationism vs. Intelligent Design: Is there a difference?" *Slate*, May 10, 2005, <http://www.slate.com/id/2118388/device/html40/workarea/3> (June 29, 2006).

6. Abby.

7. Engber.

8. "What Is Intelligent Design?"

9. Ibid.

10. Ibid.

11. Ibid.

12. Charles Darwin, *The Origin of Species: A Facsmile of the First Edition* (Cambridge, Mass.: Harvard University Press, 1964), p. 189.

13. Michael J. Behe, "Molecular Machines: Experimental Support for the Design Inference," 1997, <http://www.arn.org/docs/behe/mb_mm92496.htm> (July 25, 2006).

14. Ibid.

15. Michael Ruse, "Review of Kenneth Miller's 'Finding Darwin's God,'" *The Global Spiral*, October 26, 1999, <http://www.metanexus.net/magazine/tabid/68/id/3079/Default.aspx> (December 28, 2007).

16. "The Bacterial Flagellum," *Access Research Network*, 1998, <http://www.arn.org/docs/mm/flagellum_all.htm> (July 31, 2006).

17. "How can you tell if something is designed? Isn't that pretty subjective?" Access Research Network, n.d., <http://www.arn.org/idfaq/How%20can%20you%20tell%20if%20something%20is%20designed.htm> (April 29, 2006).

18. Ibid.

19. Lee Strobel, *The Case for a Creator* (Grand Rapids, Mich.: Zondervan, 2004), p. 282.

20. Ibid.

21. Ibid.

22. Ibid.

23. Ibid., p. 281.

24. Ibid.

25. William Dembski, "The Intelligent Design Movement," Center for Science and Culture, March 1, 1998, <http://www.discovery.org/

scripts/viewDB/index.php?command=view&id=121> (July 25, 2006).

26. Ibid.

27. Ibid.

28. Ibid.

29. Engber.

30. Dembski.

Chapter 4 The Arguments: Competing Viewpoints on Evolution and Intelligent Design

1. Edward O. Wilson, "The Consequences of Charles Darwin's 'one long argument,'" *Harvard Magazine*, November/December 2005, <http://harvardmagazine.com/2005/11/intelligent-evolution.html> (May 22, 2008).

2. Julie Sturgeon, "The great debate: evolution v. intelligent design doesn't have to pull a school district apart and leave both sides gunning for the other," *District Administration*, March 2006, p. 74.

3. Author's interview with Erica Van Dop, August 2006.

4. Robert Robb, "Origins by Court Order," *Arizona Public*, January 4, 2006, Discovery Institute News, <http://www.discovery.org/scripts/viewDB/index.php?command=view&id=3130> (February 4, 2008).

5. Jonathan Wells, "Introduction to *Icons of Evolution: Science or Myth? Why much of what we teach about evolution is wrong*," 2000, <http://www.iconsofevolution.com/intro/> (August 8, 2006).

6. Ibid.

7. Ibid.

8. Lee Strobel, *The Case for a Creator* (Grand Rapids, Mich.: Zondervan, 2004), p. 35.

9. Wells, "Introduction to *Icons of Evolution: Science or Myth? Why much of what we teach about evolution is wrong*."

10. "Intelligent Design? A special report reprinted from *Natural History* magazine," ActionBioscience.org, April 2002, <http://www.actionbioscience.org/evolution/nhmag.html> (February 4, 2008).

11. Mark Isaak, "Five Major Misconceptions about Evolution," TalkOrigins, 1995–1997, <http://www.talkorigins.org/faqs/faq-misconceptions.html> (August 29, 2006).

12. "Intelligent Design? A special report reprinted from *Natural History* magazine."

13. Sturgeon, p. 75.

14. Patrick Groff, "Letter to the Editor (The Great Debate)," *District Administration*, April 2006.

15. "Doesn't the Fossil Evidence Support Naturalistic Evolution?" Access Research Network, n.d., <http://www.arn.org/idfaq/Doesn%27t%20the%20fossil%20evidence%20support%20naturalistic%20evolution.htm> (February 4, 2008).

16. Ibid.

17. Ibid.

18. Strobel, p. 59.

19. Ibid., p. 37.

20. Jonathan Wells, "Inherit the Spin: Darwinists Answer Ten Questions with Evasions and Falsehoods," January 15, 2002, <http://www.iconsofevolution.com/embedJonsArticles.php3?id=1106> (August 8, 2006).

21. Strobel, p. 35.

22. Wells, "Inherit the Spin: Darwinists Answer 'Ten Questions' with Evasions and Falsehoods."

23. Strobel, p. 61.

24. "What about the Evidence from Embryology?" Access Research Network, n.d., <http://www.arn.org/idfaq/What%20about%20the%20evidence%20from%20embryology.htm> (April 29, 2006).

25. Ibid.

26. Ibid.

27. Strobel, p. 50.

28. Ibid.

29. Alan D. Attie, Elliot Sober, Ronald L. Numbers, et al., "Defending Science Education Against Intelligent Design: A call to action,"

Journal of Clinical Investigation, vol. 116, no. 5, May 2006, pp. 1134–1138, <http://www.jci.org/cgi/content/full/116/5/1134> (February 4, 2008).

30. Sturgeon.

31. Attie, Sober, Numbers, et al.

32. Ibid.

33. Michael Benton, "Accuracy of Fossils and Dating Methods," ActionBioscience.org, January 2001, <http://www.actionbioscience.org/evolution/benton.html> (June 21, 2006).

34. Claudia Wallis, "The Evolution Wars," *Time,* August 15, 2005, p. 26.

35. Benton.

36. Ibid.

37. Alan D. Gishlick, "Icons of Evolution? Why much of what Jonathan Wells writes about evolution is wrong," National Center for Science Education, n.d., <http://www.ncseweb.org/icons/icon1millerurey.html> (February 4, 2008).

38. Ibid.

39. Wells, "Inherit the Spin: Darwinists Answer Ten Questions With Evasions and Falsehoods."

40. Ibid.

41. Paul Z. Myers, "Haeckel's Embryos," *Icons of* Anti-*Evolution: The Essays,* n.d., <http://www.nmsr.org/text.htm#embryo> (February 4, 2008).

42. Kenneth R. Miller, "Change: Life's Grand Design," *PBS,* n.d., <http://www.pbs.org/wgbh/evolution/change/grand/index.html> (August 26, 2006).

43. "Interview: Richard Dawkins," *PBS,* n.d., <http://www.pbs.org/faithandreason/transcript/dawk-body.html> (August 26, 2006).

44. Ibid.

45. Strobel, p. 42.

46. Jonathan Wells, "Evolution by Design Succeeds Where Darwin Fails," *The World and I,* March 1998.

47. Archbishop Joseph F. Naumann, "Keep Philosophies Out of the

Classroom—Or Let Both In," *The Leaven*, February 24, 2006, <http://www.discovery.org/scripts/viewDB/index.php?command= view&id=3317> (April 14, 2006).

48. Strobel, pp. 65–66.

49. Sturgeon.

50. Wallis.

51. Sturgeon.

52. Jonathan Sarfati with Michael Matthews, "Argument: Evolution is *true* science, not 'just a theory'" (from *Refuting Evolution 2*, Chapter 3) Answers in Genesis, 2006, <http://www. answersingenesis.org/home/area/RE2/chapter3.asp> (August 23, 2006).

53. Isaak.

54. Tim M. Berra, "Separating Religious Fundamentalist 'Science' from Science," ActionBioscience.org, January 2001, <http://www.actionbioscience.org/education/berra.html> (June 21, 2006).

55. "But Doesn't Intelligent Design Refer to Something Supernatural?" Access Research Network, n..d., <http://www.arn.org/idfaq/Doesn%27t%20Intelligent%20Design %20refer%20to%20something%20supernatural.htm> (April 29, 2006).

56. Ibid.

Chapter 5 The Battleground: Evolution and Intelligent Design in Education

1. Rebecca Phillips and Dena Ross, "Beliefwatch: Camping," *Newsweek*, July 17, 2006, *MSNBC.com*, <http://www.msnbc.msn. com/id/13774258/site/newsweek/print/1/displaymode/1098> (August 1, 2006).

2. Ibid.

3. Ibid.

4. Casey Luskin, "All Sides of the Issue Belong in the Classroom," *Philadelphia Inquirer*, September 28, 2005, Discovery Institute

News, September 28, 2005, <http://www.discovery.org/scripts/viewDB/index.php?command=view&id=2898> (August 2, 2006).

5. "Court tosses Pa. school district's intelligent-design policy," First Amendment Center, December 20, 2005, <http://www.firstamendmentcenter.org/news.aspx?id=16216> (January 26, 2006).

6. Stephen Gey, "Kitzmiller: An Intelligent Ruling on 'Intelligent Design,'" *Jurist Legal News & Research*, December 29, 2005, <http://jurist.law.pitt.edu/forumy/2005/12/kitzmiller-intelligent-ruling-on.php> (January 26, 2006).

7. Robert Robb, "Origins by Court Order," *Arizona Republic*, January 4, 2006, Discovery Institute News, <http://www.discovery.org/scripts/viewDB/index.php?command=view&id=3130> (February 4, 2008).

8. Ibid.

9. Ibid.

10. Ibid.

11. "Introduction to the Establishment Clause of the First Amendment," Famous Trials Web site, n.d.,<http://www.law.umkc.edu/faculty/projects/ftrials/conlaw/estabinto.htm> (April 22, 2006).

12. Ibid.

13. Ibid.

14. Doug Linder, "Exploring Constitutional Conflicts: Free Exercise of Religion," n.d., <http://www.law.umkc.edu/faculty/projects/ftrials/conlaw/freeexercise.htm> (December 27, 2007).

15. Dave Roland, "Academic freedom: Overview," First Amendment Center, n.d., <http://www.firstamendmentcenter.org/speech/pubcollege/topic.aspx?topic=academic_freedom&SearchString=dave_roland> (August 2, 2006).

16. Robert E. Kofahl, "Scientific Evidence Against Evolution and for Creation Should Be Included in Science Curricula," in Mary E. Williams, ed., *Education: Opposing Viewpoints* (San Diego: Greenhaven Press, 2000).

17. Don Closson, "Student Rights," Probe Ministries, n.d., <http://www. probe.org/content/view/878/88> (August 2, 2006).

18. Ibid.

19. Author's interview with [name withheld], July 2006.

20. Laurie Goodstein, "A web of faith, law and science in evolution suit," *The New York Times*, September 26, 2005, p. A1(L).

21. Author's interview with Josh Van Dop, August 2006.

22. National Science Teachers Association, "Creationism Should Be Excluded from Science Courses," Mary E. Williams, ed., *Education: Opposing Viewpoints* (San Diego: Greenhaven Press, 2005).

23. Ibid.

24. "Of Pandas and People: The Central Question of Biological Origins," Foundation of Thought and Ethics, n.d., <http://www. fteonline.com/pandas-people.html> (December 28, 2007).

25. Stephen C. Meyer and Mark Hartwig, "A Note to Teachers," Discovery Institute, May 1, 1993, <http://www.discovery.org/ scripts/viewDB/index.php?command=view&id=1671&program= CSC&printerFriendly=true> (December 28, 2007).

26. Ibid.

27. Kenneth R. Miller, "*Of Pandas and People*—A Brief Critique," n.d., <http://www.kcfs.org/pandas.html> (December 28, 2007).

28. Ibid.

29. Ibid.

30. Nick Matzke, "*Of Pandas and People*, the foundation work of the 'Intelligent Design' movement," National Center for Science Education, November 23, 2004, <http://www.ncseweb.org/ resources/articles/8442_1_introduction_iof_pandas__11_23_2004. asp> (December 28, 2007).

31. "Biology books missing big picture, survey says," *CNN.com*, July 5, 2000, <http://cnnstudentnews.cnn.com/2000/fyi/teacher. resources/education.news/07/05/bio.textbooks/> (February 4, 2008).

32. Ibid.

33. Kofahl.

34. Ibid.

35. Ibid.

36. Luskin.

Chapter 6 The Players: Political Aspects of the Debate

1. Peter Baker and Peter Slevin, "Bush Remarks on 'Intelligent Design' Theory Fuel Debate," *The Washington Post*, August 3, 2005, <http://www.washingtonpost.com/wp-dyn/content/article/2005/08/02/AR2005080201686.html> (July 18, 2006).

2. Ibid.

3. John Roach, "Does 'Intelligent Design' Threaten the Definition of Science?" *National Geographic News*, April 27, 2005, <http://news.nationalgeographic.com/news/2005/04/0427_050427_intelligent_design.html> (July 18, 2006).

4. Ibid.

5. Author's interview with [name withheld].

6. Ibid.

7. Carl Weiland, "AiG's Views on the Intelligent Design Movement," Answers in Genesis, August 30, 2002, <www.answersingenesis.org/docs2002/0830_IDM.asp> (February 4, 2008).

8. Jon Hurdle, "Politics, religion drive evolution debate," *MSNBC.com*, February 10, 2005, <http://www.msnbc.msn.com/id/6948092/print/1/displaymode/1098/> (August 1, 2006).

9. Jonathan Witt, "What Are Darwinists So Afraid of?" *World Net Daily*, July 27, 2006, Discovery Institute News, <http://www.discovery.org/scripts/viewDB/index.php?command=view&id=3674> (August 2, 2006).

10. Michael Balter, "Let intelligent design and science rumble," *Los Angeles Times*, October 2, 2005, Discovery Institute News, <http://www.discovery.org/scripts/viewDB/index.php?command=view&id=2912> (February 4, 2008).

11. Ibid.

12. Ibid.

13. Ibid.

14. Pete Chadwell, "Explain Evolution's Weakness," *Bend Bulletin*, July 3, 2006, Discovery Institute News, <http://www.discovery.org/scripts/viewDB/index.php?command=view&id=3634> (February 4, 2008).

15. Ibid.

16. Stephen C. Meyer, "Teach the Controversy," *Cincinnati Enquirer*, March 30, 2002, <http://www.discovery.org/scripts/viewDB/index.php?command=view&id=1134> (February 4, 2008).

17. Phillip E. Johnson, *Defeating Darwinism by Opening Minds* (Downers Grove, Ill.: InterVarsity Press, 1997), p. 92.

18. Ibid., pp. 92–93

19. Phillip Johnson, "The Wedge of Truth: Splitting the Foundations of Naturalism," January 1, 2006, Center for Science and Culture, Discovery Institute, <http://www.discovery.org/scripts/viewDB/index.php?command=view&id=3600> (August 2, 2006).

20. John A. Boehner, Judd Gregg, and Rick Santorum, Letter to Bruce Chapman of the Discovery Institute (regarding Santorum language), <http://www.discovery.org/scripts/viewDB/index.php?command=view&id=2103> (February 4, 2008).

21. Ibid.

22. Ibid.

23. "Is There a Federal Mandate to Teach Intelligent Design Creationism?" National Center for Science Education, n.d., <http://ncseweb.org/resources/articles/ID-activists-guide-v1.pdf> (February 4, 2008).

24. Ibid.

25. Ralph Blumenthal, "Evolution's Backers in Kansas Start Counterattack," *The New York Times*, August 1, 2006, <http://www.nytimes.com/2006/08/01/us/01evolution.html?pagewanted=print> (February 4, 2008).

26. "Evolution opponents lose control of Kan. education board," First Amendment Center, August 2, 2006, <http://www.firstamendmentcenter.org/news.aspx?id=17230> (August 2, 2006).

27. Ibid.

28. Jodi Rudoren, "Ohio Expected to Rein in Class Linked to Intelligent Design," *The New York Times*, February 14, 2006, <http://www.nytimes.com/2006/02/14/education/14evolution.html?ex=1297573200&en=5fac7783b154c8e6&ei=5088&partner=rssnyt&emc=rss> (May 22, 2008).

29. Ibid.

30. Ibid.

31. "California District to Stop Teaching 'Intelligent Design,'" *CNN.com*, January 17, 2006, <http://www.cnn.com/2006/EDUCATION/01/17/evolution.debate.ap/index.html> (January 26, 2006).

32. "Calif. School District Agrees to Stop Teaching Intelligent Design," First Amendment Center, January 18, 2006, <http://www.firstamendmentcenter.org/news.aspx?id=16324> (August 2, 2006).

33. Hurdle.

Chapter 7 The End Game: What the Future Holds

1. Edward B. Davis, "Debating Darwin: The 'Intelligent Design' Movement," *The Christian Century*, July 15–22, 1998, pp. 678–681.

2. David L. Hudson Jr., "Strife over evolution, creationism predicted to continue," First Amendment Center, March 30, 2006, <http://www.firstamendmentcenter.org//news.aspx?id=16705&SearchString=evolution> (August 2, 2006).

3. Shawn McCarthy, "Does God wear a lab coat? The latest round in the culture wars pits Christians advocating intelligent design against secular parents who want kids taught evolution only. Is there a middle ground?" *Globe & Mail* (Toronto, Canada), October 1, 2005, p. F3.

4. Ibid.

5. Hudson Jr.

6. Ibid.

7. Kendrick Frazier, "U.S. 'out on a limb by ourselves' in evolution rejection, Jon Miller tells AAAS," *Skeptical Inquirer*, May–June 2006, <http://findarticles.com/p/articles/mi_m2843/is_3_30/ai_n16418725> (February 4, 2008).

8. Ibid.

9. Ibid.

10. Scott O. Lilienfeld, "Why scientists shouldn't be surprised by the popularity of intelligent design: perspectives from psychology," *Skeptical Inquirer*, May–June 2006, <http://findarticles.com/p/articles/mi_m2843/is_3_30/ai_n16418744> (February 4, 2008).

11. Sid Perkins, "Evolution in action: the trials and tribulations of intelligent design," *Science News*, February 25, 2006, <http://findarticles.com/p/articles/mi_m2843/is_8_169/ai_n16129839> (February 4, 2008).

12. Author's interview with Erica Van Dop, August 2006.

13. Marina Murphy, "Creationism looks set to evolve," *Chemistry and Industry*, March 6, 2006, p. 10.

14. Ibid.

15. Lilienfeld.

16. Stefan Lovgren, "Evolution and Religion Can Coexist, Scientists Say," *National Geographic News*, October 18, 2004, <http://news.nationalgeographic.com/news/2004/10/1018_041018_science_religion.html> (July 18, 2006).

17. "Science and Religion: Interview with Kenneth R. Miller," ActionBioscience.org, December 2004, <http://www.actionbioscience.org/evolution/miller.html> (June 14, 2006).

18. Lovgren.

19. Ibid.

20. Jonathan Wells, "Evolution and Intelligent Design" June 1, 1997, <http://www.iconsofevolution.com/embedJonsArticles.php3?id=77> (February 4, 2008).

21. Gerald Graff, "To Debate or Not to Debate Intelligent Design," *Inside Higher Education*, September 28. 2005, <http://www.insidehighered.com/views/2005/09/28/graff> (February 4, 2008).

22. Ibid.

23. Charles Haynes, "'Teaching the controversy' over evolution could be disastrous," First Amendment Center, October 27, 2002, <http://www.freedomforum.org/templates/document.asp?documentID=17157> (February 4, 2008).

24. Ibid.

25. Ibid.

26. Ibid.

Glossary

academic freedom—The freedom to pursue knowledge wherever it may lead without undue or unreasonable interference.

amendment—A change or revision to something that already exists.

American Civil Liberties Union (ACLU)—An organization founded in 1920 to protect individuals' constitutional rights.

Cambrian explosion—A term that intelligent design theorists use to describe the Cambrian period of the fossil record because so many animals appeared all at once.

creationism—A set of beliefs based on the idea that a Supreme Being (usually God) brought all life on Earth into existence through a direct act of creation; story of creation is told in the first book of the Bible called Genesis.

curriculum—A set of topics taught within a subject.

Darwinism—Controversial aspect of the theory of evolution that involves natural selection and random mutation; named after Charles Darwin and sometimes called Darwinian evolution.

dogma—A belief or set of beliefs that a political, philosophical, or moral group holds to be true.

embryo—Animal in its earliest stages of development.

Establishment Clause—A clause in the Constitution that prohibits the government from establishing a national religion or preferring one religion over another; sometimes called "separation of church and state."

eugenics—The presumed advancement of a group through selective breeding, so that the "unfit" are discouraged from reproducing while the "fit" are encouraged to reproduce.

evolution—A process of change over time; most commonly used to describe how life on Earth was formed; the idea that all living things evolved from a single organism through a series of natural processes is called the theory of evolution.

fossils—Hardened forms of things that were once living and are often used as evidence of evolution.

Free Exercise Clause—A clause in the Constitution that has been interpreted to include two freedoms—the freedom to believe and the freedom to act on that belief.

genetic drift—One of the basic mechanisms of evolution; due to chance, some living things may leave behind a few more descendents than other living things; as a result, these living things inherit some of the genes of the previous generation, regardless of their benefit or purpose.

genetics—Science involving the study of how features are passed on to other generations.

heritable—Capable of being passed on from parents to offspring through genetic material.

hypothesis—An educated guess about the outcome of an experiment or an observation.

intelligent design—A theory used to explain the complexity of living things; says that certain features of the world are more likely to occur from an intelligent cause rather than undirected natural processes.

irreducible complexity—An idea held by intelligent design theorists that certain things are complex and that all the interacting parts are needed to function; they believe an organism's complexity is an indication of design in nature.

law—In science, a law is a statement of fact that is accepted to be true, such as the law of gravity.

materialistic evolution—An idea or philosophy that implies that material, or matter, is all there is and there is no need for intelligent design or God; sometimes called naturalistic evolution.

Miller-Urey experiment—An experiment by a scientist named Stanley Miller who shot electricity through an atmosphere similar to what early Earth was believed to be like; the experiment resulted in amino acids, the building blocks of life.

modern synthesis—An idea that combines Darwin's theory of natural selection with Mendel's theory of heredity; this idea says that natural selection, mutation, genetic drift, and other natural processes cause the changes in populations over time.

mutation—A change in DNA, the hereditary material of life, that is random; it can be beneficial, neutral, or harmful for an organism.

natural selection—The primary way in which evolutionary changes happen.

neo-Darwinism—The modern approach to Darwin's original theory, which says that favorable variations occur by both natural selection and random mutation.

pseudoscience—Not truly a science, but a "fake" science.

Santorum language—Ideas about how evolution should be taught that are conveyed in a conference report attached to the No Child Left Behind Act; the ideas are meant to be a guide but are not required.

social Darwinism—Idea that says human society is a battleground known as "survival of the fittest"; as a result, the fittest become the richest and own the most property.

specified complexity—A method used to determine whether or not something is the result of an intelligent designer; it occurs when the odds are extremely low that something could have happened by chance and when the object or event matches a recognizable pattern.

teach the controversy—A political-action campaign designed to promote teaching "all the evidence" relating to evolutionary theory; calls for schools to equip students with the ability to critically analyze evolutionary theory.

theistic evolution—Idea that accepts evidence that the earth is billions of years old and that evolution can explain much of history—but not the creation of the human soul.

theory—A well-substantiated explanation of the natural world; can include facts, laws, inferences, and tested hypotheses; supported by evidence and can be tested; sometimes used to make predictions.

trait—A quality or characteristic of an organism.

vertebrate embryo—An animal with a segmented spinal column and a well-developed brain.

The Wedge—This strategy, formally called The Wedge of Truth, is used by scholars to cast doubt on the philosophical aspects of Darwinism; the name comes from a method used for splitting logs.

For More Information

Evolution

American Association for the
Advancement of Science
1200 New York Avenue NW
Washington, DC 20005
202-326-6400

National Academy of Sciences
500 Fifth Street NW
Washington, DC 20001
202-334-2000

National Biology Teachers
Association
12030 Sunrise Valley Drive
Suite 110
Reston, VA 20191
703-264-9696 or 800-406-0775

National Center for Science
Education
420 Fortieth Street, Suite 2
Oakland, CA 94609-2509
510-601-7203

National Science Teachers Association
1840 Wilson Boulevard
Arlington, VA 22201
703-243-7100

Intelligent Design

Access Research Network
P.O. Box 38069
Colorado Springs, CO 80937-8069
719-633-1772

Discovery Institute
1511 Third Avenue, Suite 808
Seattle, WA 98101
206-292-0401

Foundation for Thought and Ethics
P.O. Box 830721
Richardson, TX 75083-0721

Intelligent Design Network
P.O. Box 14702
Shawnee Mission, KA 66285
913-268-0852

International Society for Complexity,
Information, and Design
66 Witherspoon Street, Suite 1800
Princeton, NJ 08542
609-924-4424

Other

American Civil Liberties Union
125 Broad Street, 18th Floor
New York, NY 10004

Americans United for the Separation
of Church and State
518 C Street NE
Washington, DC 20002
202- 466-3234

First Amendment Center (at
Vanderbilt University)
1207 Eighteenth Avenue South
Nashville, TN 37212
615-727-1600

Further Reading

Pro-Evolution Books

Isaak, Mark. *The Counter-Creationism Handbook.* Westport, Conn.: Greenwood Press, 2005.

Skybreak, Andrea. *The Science of Evolution and the Myth of Creationism: Knowing What's Real and Why It Matters.* Chicago: Insight Press, 2006.

Pro–Intelligent Design Books

Johnson, Phillip E. *Defeating Darwinism by Opening Minds.* Downers Grove, Ill.: InterVarsity Press, 1997.

Strobel, Lee. *The Case for a Creator: A Journalist Investigates Scientific Evidence That Points Toward God.* Grand Rapids, Mich.: Zondervan Publishing, 2004.

Other

Braun, Eric, editor. *Creationism vs. Evolution.* San Diego: Greenhaven Press, 2006.

Hansen, Freya Ottem. *The Scopes Monkey Trial: A Headline Court Case.* Berkeley Heights, N.J.: Enslow Publishers, Inc., 2000.

Moore, Randy. *Evolution in the Courtroom: A Reference Guide.* Santa Barbara, Calif.: ABC-CLIO, 2002.

Internet Addresses

Access Research Network
(Frequently Asked Questions About Intelligent Design)
<http://www.arn.org/id_faq.htm>

Understanding Evolution
(Evolution 101)
<http://evolution.berkeley.edu/evolibrary/article/evo_01>

First Amendment Center
<http://www.firstamendmentcenter.org/>

Index